Tracks Across the Landscape

Tracks Across the Landscape

THE S&L COMMEMORATIVE HISTORY

BRIAN CAMPBELL

with A.J.B. Johnston

University College of Cape Breton Press
Box 5300
Sydney, Nova Scotia
CANADA B1P 6L2

Book design by Brenda Berry, Goose Lane Editions.
Unless otherwise noted the photographs are the property of the S&L Archives.
Printed and bound in Canada by Advocate Printing, Pictou, Nova Scotia.

Storytellers and Informants: Charlie Bagnell, Ivan Bates, Allan Campbell, Jack DeCourcy, Cletus Egan, Leo Evans, Guy Hiltz, Ralph Humphrey, Doug MacCormick, Bill MacDonald, Joe R. MacDonald, Lauchie A. MacDonald, Rod MacDonald, Harvey MacLeod, Stan MacRury, Gerald Norris, John O'Neill and Rose O'Neill

Illustration Editor: Eugene Magee

Publication Committee: William Bussey, Margie Cameron, Jean Kyte and William O'Shea

Canadian Cataloguing in Publication Data
Campbell, Brian, 1947 -
Tracks across the landscape
Includes bibliographical references.

ISBN 0-920336-64-7

1. Sydney & Louisburg Railway — History.
2. Railroads — Nova Scotia — Cape Breton Island — History. I. Johnston. A.J.B. II. Title
HE2810-S93C36 1995 385'.06'57169 C95-950081-2

For the men and women
of the Sydney & Louisburg Railway,
and their families

Acknowledgments

We acknowledge with appreciation the assistance of the following organizations or agencies:

Enterprise Cape Breton Corporation

Louisbourg Heritage Society

Town of Louisbourg

The Louisbourg 1995 Commemoration Society

and the individuals who contributed in any way to the successful completion of this project.

Born in Sydney, Brian Campbell has worked in the heritage field for years, publishing on different aspects of Cape Breton history.

John Johnston is the author of numerous studies of 18th-century Louisbourg.

Eugene Magee, curator of the S & L Railway Museum since 1990.

Contents

CHAPTER FOUR
Slow But Steady: A Decade Of Growth 1883-93

CHAPTER FIVE
The S&L Arrives, It's 1895

CHAPTER SIX
The S&L Line And Its Heyday

CHAPTER SEVEN

The End . . . and a Beginning

APPENDIX A

Locomotives

APPENDIX B

Chronology

CHAPTER ONE

Lasting Memories

The development of the Sydney and Louisburg Railway, like the tracks it laid across the landscape, followed a winding course through Cape Breton's history. For well over half a century, the S&L Railway played a pivotal and memorable role in the life of the island.

For seven decades the S&L supported and sustained the industries, businesses, and people of the northeastern corner of Cape Breton Island. Once it was among the most active freight lines in Canada, a fact that belied its nickname, the "Slow and Lazy." Its main responsibility — its principal achievement — was that it carried tens of thousands of tons of coal to their place of export. At the same time, it moved hundreds of industrial-area workers to and from their places of work.

Along the way and over the years the S&L also touched the lives of thousands of ordinary Cape Bretoners. These were people who had little or nothing to do with coal or industry. Day-shoppers, berry-pickers, sight-seers, tourists, people on their way to dances or loved ones — all made use of the S&L. Some took advantage of the regularly scheduled runs. Others travelled on extra trains supplied for a variety of events; these were referred to as "specials." They ran most commonly during the summer and were used by people going to their cottages on the Mira, or to picnics, or to festivals at Louisbourg.

The miners' picnic on the Mira River was one regular summer event that called for many rail cars carrying hundreds of passengers who delighted in the idea of having a day in the country. Rose O'Neill is one of many who fondly recall these outings. It was 1913 and it was her first picnic: "I can still remember the excitement as I was lifted up into the boxcar." Coach cars were provided for some of the adults, but the children rode in windowless box cars outfitted for the occasion. "They had plank seats down the sides. Like every kid, I was dying to see out; but I couldn't do that." A fellow was posted at the box car door to keep an

Where's the 'o'?
Louisbourg and Louisburg. The historic French settlement and the modern Town of Louisbourg are both spelled with the "o". For most of the 19th and well into the 20th century, however, the "o" was not used. It was during that period that the S&L Railway came to life. Thus, one spells the railway's name as the Sydney and Louisburg, *sans* the "o".

#87, an 0-8-0 belches a cloud of smoke and soot as it rounds a turn with a coal train. *[S&LRHSoc.]*

eye on the children. "We had to sit down." The stern atmosphere of the ride to the picnic ultimately increased the enjoyment of the outing itself, once the destination had been reached.

Typically, there was a casual informality about the S&L that made it beloved by its passengers. Without much difficulty, or so it would seem, people would flag the train down and get on board. Theoretically there was the question of the fare. Yet it appears there were more than a few who enjoyed a 'free ride.' One oldtimer tells the story of offering to pay, but being rebuffed. He was informed: "You've never paid before and we're not going to break a perfect record." Another recollection is that of Allan Campbell, who grew up to work as chief despatcher for the S&L. As a youngster, Mr. Campbell recalls handing his ticket money to conductor Michael "Big Mick" MacKenzie. In a single motion, Big Mick would take the money, place it in his pocket momentarily, give a wink, then hand the fare back to young Allan. A few pennies went a long way in those days, and Big Mick's slight of hand brought a large smile to a young face.

The S&L Railway was also there at times of crisis, or in an emergency. When the need arose, on short notice, day or night, the rail company would volunteer an engine and rail car to transport a critically ill patient to a hospital in Sydney or Glace Bay.

Still, one does not want to romanticize excessively the era of the S&L. Picturesque as its billows of steam may now seem to have been, one needs to remember that the smoke was not healthy for those who breathed it. One method of doing a quick start-up in the locomotives was to use old railway ties, topped off with a liberal amount of waste oil. A match put the ties alight, and they could belch out quite a chemical cocktail. Neither that smoke nor the regular cloud of coal smoke was welcomed by people with light-coloured houses, nor by ladies who had just hung out their laundry!

One also needs to remember that not all the involvements and stories of the S&L turned out to be happy ones. There were some undeniable bumps in the road. There was a major wreck on the Mira River in 1903. And there were numerous other accidents and mishaps. Some injuries were minor — what might be called "routine"; others much more traumatic.

The S&L even found itself playing an inevitable role in one of the more well-known disputes in Cape Breton's labour history, the difficult and sorrowful strike by coal miners in 1925. During the strife, miner William Davis was shot and killed. It so happened that it was the S&L Railway that carried the coal to the power plant at Waterford Lake that was supplying electricity to the mines during the strike. Lauchie MacDonald recalls being in the cab when the train was suddenly surrounded by angry miners. One man entered the cab with what looked like an axe handle. He was eventually persuaded to leave the cab, and Lauchie was relieved that he had been able to keep the engine under full steam throughout the wait, just in case the engineer gave the order to leave.

For 70 years the winding and weaving line of the S&L Railway was one of the threads of local society, helping to stitch together the communities it linked. "Slow and Lazy" it may have been, but "Sure and Loved" it became.

"Just at the Pier roundhouse, we had the stoker engines and they'd make black smoke like you never saw. You'd put the stoker on there on three of four of those engines warming up for the shift and the smoke would be rolling up. You couldn't even see the houses up on the hill above there for the smoke! No one ever said a word. But I can remember coming from the Pier past the houses along the tracks on Railroad Street. I had one of the stoker engines — #101 — she was a dirty engine — stuff flying out of the stack and everything. I can remember a woman hanging out her washing on the clothesline there and waving a baseball bat at me! She'd have killed you if she got a chance. But when you were hauling out of the Pier, it was uphill and you just had to pour on the coals."

— JACK DECOURCY, who joined the S&L in 1949, and is soon to retire from the DEVCO Railway after 46 years as a railroader

❖ ❖ ❖

MEMORABLE ACCIDENTS

I saw one bad one up in the coal yard. I wasn't there at the time but the next morning, I was there. It was the time a young fellow got his leg jammed between two trains in the Pier yard. They came up through the long siding on #1 I think it was. They came in with a train of coal and the young fella was on the footboard and jeez, he got caught in between the two trains and he was there all night and he was still conscious, never went out at all. He was jammed in there. His legs were crushed to pieces. Oh, there was an awful rush then to try to get him free. Next morning when I came out the ambulance was up there and I rushed right up to see what was going on and this was what was facing me. I was section foreman. So I had a burner [welding torch]. You know the cow catcher on the front of the diesel. We had to burn that whole cow catcher right off and it was the fireman . . . that came up and I had the burner and he had to burn that whole thing right off before they lifted that fella out of it. And he was still conscious. But I guess they were putting needles to him and everything else. The doctor was right there with him. But soon as they got him out of there and put him in the ambulance, he went black out then you know. But he lost his leg. He was a brakeman from Glace Bay. Young fella.

—IVAN BATES, speaking of one of the more memorable accidents he had seen on the S&L line

The S&L line continued to play major roles for both freight and passengers throughout the 1950s and into the 1960s. In 1951, for instance, the railway took delivery of 100 new hopper cars, bringing its total fleet up to 1050. The yearly freight totals hauled on the line during the 1950s were in the range of 4 million tons. There were still 400 people employed at the time, and 31 locomotives on the S&L roster. That is not to say that everything was "modern." Far from it, and that indeed was part of the S&L's charm. One of the engines still in service in 1959 had been manufactured in 1891.

Though it resisted for many years, the S&L eventually felt obliged to move into the era of diesel. In 1960 the S&L company bought its first diesel-powered locomotives. One year later, the era of steam was finally over once and for all. On November 17, 1961, the last two coal-powered engines on the line, No. 88 and No. 90, made their last runs.

For a few more years the S&L railway remained in business, using its new diesel engines to haul cargoes like salt to the fish plants of Louisbourg. It had become uneconomical to haul coal to the Louisbourg pier any longer. World markets for coal disappeared as the then much less-expensive oil and gas became the dominant energy sources during the late 1950s and throughout the 1960s. The S&L line was a local casualty of the world-wide trend.

In 1963, after nearly 70 memorable years of carrying workers, picnickers, and shoppers, the passenger service of the S&L was discontinued. Five years later, the federal government passed legislation to create the Cape Breton Development Corporation (DEVCO). The legislation contained no provision for the maintenance of a rail line to Louisbourg. Instead, the S&L Railway was absorbed as a small part of the coal division of DEVCO. The rail division was re-named the DEVCO Railway. Within months, the tracks to Louisbourg were lifted and sold for their scrap value. With that, the S&L's run through Cape Breton history was finally over.

In the pages that follow we explore the story of the S&L Railway. We look at the line, the trains, and the people. Not just those who built and financed it, but the ordinary folk who day-in and day-out made it run. The S&L may only be a memory, but a fond one.

CHAPTER TWO

Before The Railways

During the late 19th and early 20th centuries railways came to be the dominant form of transportation on the North American continent. Cape Breton Island was not untouched by the phenomenon.

How the railways came to the island — in particular the S&L — can be a rather long story. An abbreviated version is offered here.

When Coal was King

Like so many Cape Breton enterprises, the first railways on the island owed their existence largely to coal. The S&L was no exception.

By the middle of the 19th century, energy in cheap and abundant supply was a key to prosperity. As the engines of industry multiplied across North America and Europe, they developed an almost insatiable demand for energy in all its forms. Fortune smiled on only a few places, where a source of fuel was readily available and able to be exploited. In Texas and the mid-Western United States, energy could be pumped from the ground as crude oil. On Cape Breton Island, the fuel was coal.

At least as far back as the 1600s, and probably much earlier, supplies were being chipped from outcrops along the coast. London diarist Samuel Pepys mentions Cape Breton coal in a September 1687 entry. Decades earlier, French explorer and trader Nicolas Denys took samples of the valued mineral back to France. As early as 1677 Paris was imposing a duty on every ton of coal mined on the island. After the settlement of Louisbourg in 1713, the practice continued. By 1720, the French were mining coal on a regular basis at Port Morien

"There are mines of coal through the whole extent of my concession near the seashore, of a quality equal to the Scotch, which I have proved at various times on the spot, and also in France where I have brought them for trials."
— NICOLAS DENYS, 1672

❖ ❖ ❖

(Cow Bay). Though never a major operation, there was enough mined that visitors to Louisbourg, including New Englanders, bought small quantities for their own use, or to sell back in their home ports.

With the defeat of the French at Louisbourg in 1758, Great Britain gained control of Cape Breton Island. It fell to government surveyors — men like Samuel Holland and J.F.W. DesBarres — to confirm the vastness of the deposits. Yet the seams were not to be developed extensively, at least not by private developers. The British crown retained exclusive ownership over mining rights, including those for coal.

War with the United States in 1812, fluctuations in mining royalties and markets, and a host of other difficulties meant that none of the early Cape Breton mining operations flourished. Production rarely exceeded 10,000 tons a year. A dramatic turnabout began in 1827.

In an earlier exercise of royal prerogative, George III had given his son exclusive rights to the mineral wealth of Nova Scotia. The Duke of York had lived like a king without much hope of ever actually gaining the crown. He accumulated massive debts. As part of a settlement with creditors, the duke handed over a 69-year lease on the mineral rights to Cape Breton Island and mainland Nova Scotia. The transaction resulted in the formation of the General Mining Association [G.M.A.].

For three decades the G.M.A. produced thousands of tons of coal on the island. Yet its restrictive monopoly was deeply resented as it inhibited the development of additional mines. After considerable struggle and debate, the G.M.A.'s monopoly ended in 1858. Soon after, other coal companies were formed. Production could now soar.

The Transportation Problem

To move the large quantity of coal that could be mined on Cape Breton there would have to be an efficient system of transportation. Essentially that meant railways and ships. At first, the rails were made of wood and horses provided the power. In time, steel rails replaced wooden ones and steam locomotives gave horsepower a whole new meaning. Soon it was clear that a network of railroads had to be built to connect the collieries to tidewater.

In 1870, the International Coal and Railway Company constructed a standard gauge line between Bridgeport and the International Piers at Sydney. A year later, the Cape Breton Company Limited began operating a narrow gauge line from Reserve to a 600-foot pier on Sydney harbour, a distance of 12 1/2 miles. Built under the direction of F.N. Gisborne, the line was part of a consolidation of the Reserve, Balmoral, Lorway, Emery and Schooner Pond collieries. The efficiencies achieved were enormous. The output from several mines could be moved from the coal face to the coal pier in a continuous operation.

The system, however, had one major drawback. All shipments ground to a halt when winter set in and Sydney's harbour filled with ice. What was needed was an ice-free port, a winter shipping terminus. If Sydney didn't fill the bill, then what harbour would? The answer, to those who knew their history, lay not far away.

> *[In the 1880s] . . . there were no railroads on Cape Breton connecting with the mainland . . . There were two railways of ten miles connecting Sydney with the mines. There were five or six different companies operating collieries here, shipping from six to seven months from Sydney harbour. The output was so limited that we looked with anxious eyes at any schooner coming into the harbour to see whether she would come to us or to the rival colliery . . . In the early nineties the mines now owned by the Dominion Coal Company had only reached an output of some 800,000 or 900,000 tons. There was not much to do in the winter, and we used to meet at each other's houses and talk over what we would do when the mythical American syndicate came along with many millions of dollars in their pockets.*
>
> —J.S. MCLENNAN, after-dinner speech, 1900

CHAPTER THREE

An Idea Becomes A Railway

An Ice-Free Port

For five decades in the 18th century Cape Breton Island had been Ile Royale, a French colony whose principal settlement was Louisbourg. Best-known as a fortress, Louisbourg was also a seaport. And a largely ice-free seaport at that. As a port 150 years earlier Louisbourg had been one of the busiest in North America, ranking just behind the major American colonial ports. Huge quantities of dried cod were exported from its harbour to Europe and the West Indies. Now, in the late 19th century, planners turned toward Louisbourg. They wondered if the same seaport could now send coal rather than codfish to faraway markets? The challenge of course was to get the coal to the town, to the shore of the harbour. That's where a railway would come in.

The Idea Developed, 1874

It was an English-born engineer, Frederick Gisborne, who came up with the solution to the coal industry's perennial shipping problems. That is, he was the first to take practical steps to extend a railway to Louisbourg. Others may have had the idea before him, but Gisborne had the wherewithal (not to mention the financial backers) to make it happen.

And so the project to build a railway to Louisbourg was begun. It would have been a formidable task under the best conditions. The task was made that much more difficult by the rugged terrain. The proposed route had to pass over 21 miles of brooks and ravines, a river, and assorted swamps and marshes. Luckily, Gisborne was not intimidated. He was used to adversity, having completed some of the Maritime's earliest telegraph systems, including North America's first submarine cable (between Prince Edward Island and New Brunswick).

The Cape Breton Company, with Gisborne as its manager, set out to raise capital in Great Britain. Their advertising material, published in 1875, promoted Louisbourg as both the eastern port for all Canadian mail and as a coaling depot for Atlantic steamers. A trading system was proposed that would see Louisbourg as the hub of a vast network, an updated version of what the fortress town had been in the days of French colonization.

In Gisborne's 19th-century vision, products from central and western Canada would be warehoused at Louisbourg, ready for distribution when markets were most favourable. Elevators would hold western wheat and grain for transshipment to European markets. Ships from Quebec and the Great Lakes would carry Cape Breton coal on their return voyage. Goods imported from the West Indies and other trading nations would be redistributed from the Louisbourg port. Extending the Intercolonial Railway to Louisbourg was raised as a possibility. It would open access to the entire eastern seaboard of the United States and to central Canada.

Variations of Gisborne's proposal were voiced many times over the next 30 years, most frequently during federal and provincial elections. Gisborne even drew up a plan for a "New Town," on Louisbourg's Havenside, to accommodate the expected influx of new development.

A Tortuous Route

A rail line does not spring to life quickly or easily. It is both time-consuming and expensive. It starts, therefore, with money. Or rather, a search for money. Investors had to be first found, then convinced the project was viable.

Work on the line from Norway Junction (Reserve) to Louisbourg began in 1874. It was, at times, a tortuous process. Labourers used the rustic but effective methods of the day to complete the roadway, crossing brooks, gorges, rock cuts and the Mira River. One meandering stream had to be spanned five times in a distance of only a few hundred yards. Along with the basic ties, rails and ballasted road bed, construction included 32 wooden trestles, 35 wooden culverts and an iron bridge across the Mira River. The bridge was fabricated in England and shipped to Cape Breton in sections. Off-loaded at Mira Bay,

The Gisborne bridge was the marvel of the Mira and is seen here with the center span removed, possibly under demolition. The bridge is said to have swayed gently under the weight of a passing train . [S&LRHSoc.]

the sections were hauled to the construction site by teams of oxen. There, at its final destination, it was reassembled to span the river, a majestic sight to the many onlookers. For Cape Breton Island, it was a technological marvel in its time.

During the construction phase, the Gisborne railway, in addition to local labour, attracted large numbers of itinerant workers. Many stayed in boarding houses along the route, one of the "spin-offs" to the local economy.

Building a railroad has never been an exact science. Construction delays and cost overruns on the Gisborne project took their toll on the company's finances. By 1877, investors were looking closely at the balance sheet. They didn't much like what they saw, a bottom line in red ink. In an attempt to reverse the decline the directors sent word to England that a new manager was needed. The call was answered, in the person of Captain David J. Kennelly.

Captain Kennelly

D.J. Kennelly was born in Ireland and educated in England as a lawyer. He later served as a naval captain, and helped personally suppress some of the revolts in India during what came to be known as the Mutiny of 1857. It was a mix of experience which gave him the reputation, upon his arrival in Cape Breton, of being tough but fair. In the rough and tumble world of 19th-century industry, Kennelly was probably well suited to the task at hand.

Captain Kennelly's attempt to save the Cape Breton Company included a program of strict austerity. He began to trim the operation by closing the Schooner Pond, Lorway and Emery coal seams. Efforts were concentrated on the Reserve to Sydney part of the company. Unconvinced that the situation was improving, nervous creditors foreclosed in 1878, seizing all mines, shipping piers, railways and mining licences. Shortly after, the assets were sold at public auction for £12,000 sterling.

Despite legal entanglements, Kennelly emerged as the new owner of the defunct Cape Breton Company. He reorganized, refinanced and renamed the business, calling it the Sydney and Louisburg Coal and Railway Company Limited.

The Line to Louisbourg — The Original S&L

With the completion of the rail line to Louisbourg and the construction of a shipping pier on the southeast side of the harbour at Havenside, the original S&L Railway cast a tall shadow over the ruins of the bygone fortress town. At the end of the line, the company built a small hotel, an engine shed, a blacksmith shop and two duplex houses for the workers. With the railway, there was finally a link to Sydney, and to the major collieries of the coal field. With access to Louisbourg's mainly ice-free harbour, it would at last be possible to ship coal and other products year-round.

D.J. Kennelly, as the manager of the railway, lived at Louisbourg in a fine home on a point of land near the harbour mouth. More than a century later, the point is still known as Kennelly Point.

Like Gisborne before him, Capt. Kennelly developed an enthusiasm for Louisbourg's potential. He adopted many of Gisborne's ideas and added his own. One was to establish an express steamship service between Louisbourg and Milford Haven, in Wales. He produced and distributed a booklet on the topic, *The Atlantic Ferry. Louisburg and Milford Haven* (London, 1901). Provided there was a rail link to New Glasgow and the eastern seaboard of the United States — which was, needless to say, a monumental provisio -Kennelly was convinced Louisbourg could rival New York as the North American terminus for trans-Atlantic passenger travel. Whether it was a scheme with any practical application or the pipe dream of an aging industrialist will never be known. The idea never got beyond the dreaming stages.

The operating life of the first S&L Railroad was short. In 1883 a forest fire swept through the area and destroyed most of the wooden bridges and trestles on the Louisbourg end of the line. The fire could not have come at a worse time. Coal markets were slack and the money for repairs was not available. As a result the line was abandoned by its owners.

During its brief existence, the original S&L had a lasting effect on the Cape Breton coal industry. It proved that winter shipping was possible and it helped make mining a more continuous operation. Louisbourg, until then a tiny fishing village, was brought into the industrial age, funnily enough by learning a lesson from the 18th-century history of the once-bustling seaport. People had a market for their labour and they achieved a degree of prosperity.

Perhaps most important from today's perspective was that the first S&L railroad accelerated a shift in settlement away from the western side of Louisbourg harbour (the site of the original fortress) to the eastern end, where most of the new building took place. Had that development taken place on the western side, as some plans called for, it would have meant that the area could not have been later developed into the National Historic Site it is today.

In the end, the fire that destroyed the rail line in 1883 proved fatal for the first S&L. There would be no phoenix rising from its ashes. At least, not for a decade.

The port of Louisburg . . . is open at all seasons of the year, and by that port we have the shortest route to Liverpool . . . 200 miles shorter than by way of Halifax, the nearest port to England we now have in Canada.

— CHARLES TUPPER, quoted in Kennelly's brochure, 1901

CHAPTER FOUR

Slow But Steady: A Decade Of Growth
1883-93

Self-sufficiency was still a hallmark of life on Cape Breton Island late in the 19th century. Most rural families and communities grew or manufactured almost everything they needed. There were dozens of small water-powered mills producing a variety of products from grains and spun wool to finished lumber. Steam tanneries provided leather for harness shops and shoe makers. Blacksmiths and tinsmiths fabricated a broad range of metal products. Sydney and North Sydney had small furniture factories. Coastal communities like Louisbourg lived mostly by the harvest of a bountiful fishery. Small fish plants and canneries dotted the coastline.

But Cape Breton's, and Nova Scotia's, sea-oriented economy went through a painful transition during the latter part of the 19th century. Shipbuilding, lumbering and fishing felt the effects of a generally depressed world economy. Worse still, new technologies like steel ships and refrigerated transport, along with changing market demands, added their negative effects. Confederation with Canada in 1867 placed much of the political power in the centre of the new country. The drive to settle western Canada and the implementation of the National Policy of Sir John A. Macdonald meant there was diminishing interest in the problems of the Maritimes. A shrinking labour market and better opportunities elsewhere led to an out-migration of 160,000 people from the region between 1861 and 1891. Atlantic Canada's "Golden age of Wood, Wind and Water", brief but illustrious, was over. People such as Gisborne and Kennelly clearly hoped that the new railway technology would usher in a new era of growth and prosperity.

A stranger has appeared in the Mira Bay in the shape of a small steamer. The first steam vessel to be seen here.

— NEHEMIAH MARTEL, resident of Mira Gut, 1867

A novel and unexpected sight appeared in the Bay today. Three steamers engaged in laying the telegraph cable from Brest to Boston have anchored in Mira River.

— NEHEMIAH MARTEL, 1869

❖ ❖ ❖

By Land and By Sea

This view of the Louisbourg Pier shows sailing ships docked alongside the new pier and a steel freighter waits to right. The Golden age of Wood, Wind and Water was over. C1895. [S&LRHSoc.]

Though 19th-century Cape Breton was a largely self-contained society, travel across it was not always easy. Roadways were extensive but not for the faint of heart. Most were rough and dusty in the summer, impassable with deep snow in the winter, and deep in mud in the spring. Overland travel to the mainland was by stagecoach to the Canso Strait, then by open ferry to Mulgrave.

The most common, and often preferred, mode of transport was by water. Cape Bretoners still had easy access to a wide variety of water transport. Scores of small fishing boats and schooners plied the inland and coastal waters. Hundreds of ocean-going sailing ships from North America and Europe called regularly at ports like Arichat, Sydney and Louisbourg.

Coal was one of the reasons the vessels came. As the shipping world made the transition from sail to steam, Cape Breton enjoyed modest growth as a coal bunkering port.

For local water travel, islanders were served by companies around the island. Each destination had a government wharf and for years before the advent of railways and all-weather roads, these waterfront facilities were the focus for much of the commercial life in coastal communities.

By the 1890s, scheduled service for off-island travel had become more frequent. The Reid Line of Newfoundland made three trips a week between Port-aux-Basques and North Sydney. Louisbourg became the winter port for these Newfoundland ships. The Black Diamond Line had five steamers connecting Cape Breton with St. John's, Newfoundland; Charlottetown, Prince Edward Island and Montreal, Quebec. Ships of the Plant and Red Cross lines followed with connections between Sydney, Halifax, St. John's, Boston and New York.

Communications

Telecommunications came early to Cape Breton. North America's first government-owned telegraph system was set up in 1849 connecting Amherst, Truro and Halifax. Two years later, it was reincorporated as the Nova Scotia Electric Telegraph, a private company. Lines were pushed eastward to Port Hood and Sydney. Across the harbour, North Sydney was chosen as the landing point for one of the first trans-Atlantic cables. It eventually became a major centre for Western Union, a facility that put Cape Breton in touch with all of North America and most of Europe.

Telegraphs and railways were closely linked, for it was a natural union. Lines and poles could be run along established rights of way and railway stations were perfectly situated for sending, receiving and distributing telegraph messages to the public. The S&L would eventually develop its own telegraphic system which made it doubly effective as a communications link for the towns it served.

The first tentative telephone conversations on the island were held in the summer of 1877. They came compliments of Gardiner Greene Hubbard, a Boston-based lawyer and businessman, and the father-in-law to inventor Alexander Graham Bell. Beginning in the 1850s, Hubbard, along with several other New Englanders, including poet Henry Wadsworth

Longfellow, acquired a number of leases in the coal fields of Cape Breton. During a tour of these properties, the Caledonia Mine at Glace Bay, Hubbard decided to test the new telephone device. Lines were run between the workings and the surface. The experiment proved successful. The following year, 1878, the General Mining Association purchased a five-station telephone system for its operations on the north side of Sydney harbour, linking the company's stores, offices, mines and railway in the area of North Sydney and Sydney Mines. The telephones of the Caledonia mine and the G.M.A. were among the first in Canada.

A decade later public telephone service came to Cape Breton when area business people bought the French Cable Company's abandoned line between Lorraine and Sydney. With a capital investment of $10,000 they established the Eastern Telephone Company. The company was well positioned to participate in what soon would be a burgeoning Cape Breton economy. By 1911, Eastern Telephone was one of four companies that merged to form Maritime Tel and Tel, the telecommunications network.

A Rail Link with the Rest of Canada

An historical milestone was reached in 1890 when the tracks of the Intercolonial Railway came to Cape Breton Island. The Halifax and Cape Breton Railway, or the Eastern Extension as it was then commonly called, reached as far as Crittenden's Creek, just outside Antigonish by 1879. The final 80 miles of track were laid the following year. From a rail head on the mainland side near Mulgrave, the ferry *Norwegian* carried passengers and freight across the Canso Strait to Point Tupper. It would be another ten years before the trans-island line was built.

The Eastern Extension was fraught with controversy from its beginning, becoming something of a political football. It fuelled a sporadic but consistently contentious debate in the Nova Scotia Legislature for almost 40 years. It even became the subject of a Royal Commission. Eventually, the decision was made to continue the railway across Cape Breton. Controversy then flared over the route the line should follow.

There were three choices under consideration. First, a southern route through St. Peters and on to Sydney and Louisbourg. Second, a northern route through Inverness and Victoria county terminating at North Sydney. The third choice was a compromise, a central line up the middle of the Island with a crossing at Grand Narrows on the Bras d'Or Lakes. Politicians and electors in the district south of the Mira River formed their own lobby and argued forcefully, alas unsuccessfully, to have Louisbourg designated as one of the terminal points for the new line.

Compromise carried the day, and the central route won out. Cape Breton folklore has it that the decision was made by Prime Minister Sir John A. Macdonald when he visited Grand Narrows for a political picnic. So impressed was Macdonald by the splendid scenery, with its striking similarity to his native Scotland, he gave the nod to that route. It makes a good story, but fierce politicking from all sides figured heavily in the mix. Local politicians did everything they could to influence the outcome. There were inevitable winners and losers with the decision, and long after it was not uncommon to hear Cape Bretoners revisit the topic, sometimes in heated debate.

The Cape Breton Railway

The Cape Breton Railway, as the extension was called, was built in two sections; first from Point Tupper to Grand Narrows, and then from the Narrows to Sydney. Builders Isbester and Reid began the first section in 1889.

Little is known about Isbester, but Reid was Robert G. Reid who had already gained a reputation as a railroad and bridge builder throughout North America. A native of the Highlands of Scotland, Reid had struck it rich in the Australian gold fields. He then turned his energies to public works construction. By the 1870s, he figured North America was the place to be, since the move toward railroad construction was at a fever pitch. Reid negotiated contracts that included the erection of the International Bridge across the Niagara River, railway bridges between Montreal and Ottawa, and the crossing of the Lachine rapids on the St. Lawrence River above Montreal. He also laid the rails around the north shore of Lake Superior. In short, he had considerable railway experience.

The Reid-Newfoundland Company, of which Reid was president, eventually came to own the railway, as well as a fleet of steamships and the telegraph system on Newfoundland.

Reid's section of the Cape Breton project went smoothly and according to plan, except at Grand Narrows. The original plan had been for a train ferry there. That idea was dropped in favour of a steel bridge, probably due to Reid's influence.

While Reid was making progress, the contractor on the second section went bankrupt, not an unusual occurrence in the world of railroad builders. The government hired Hiram Donkin to finish the task. Donkin was another experienced railroad man, having begun his career as an assistant to Sir Sanford Fleming, later known as the "father of standard time" and at one time Chief Engineer of the Nova Scotia Railway. As a junior engineer Donkin had accompanied Fleming on the original survey for the Canadian Pacific Railroad. Later in his career Donkin would become Deputy Minister of Mines for Nova Scotia. In the intervening years he was active in the industrial life of Cape Breton. As a superintendent of the Dominion Coal Company, he supervised the building of the second railway to Louisbourg.

The difficult lake and mountain terrain of central Cape Breton meant, inevitably, that the new rail line would have to be crooked, very crooked. Political satirists of the time interpreted the meandering course in a different way. They speculated that whenever the proposed route missed the farm of a government supporter, surveyors doubled back to make sure he was given a slice of the right-of-way money.

A Celebratory Run

The Cape Breton Railway was finished and ready for a trial run by the fall of 1890. On October 18 the first train — the five-coach train of Governor General Lord Stanley — arrived in Sydney. It capped a celebratory run.

Stanley's train left Halifax at midnight; arrived at Mulgrave in the early morning; was barged across the Canso Strait and coupled to ICR engine No. 166 on the new rails at Point Tupper. Near the midway point at Grand Narrows, Lord Stanley formally declared the railroad opened and took the controls himself to drive the engine across the new bridge. Groups gathered all along the route to welcome the train, which was the foremost symbol of modernity of the era. As the train rolled into Sydney at 7:10 pm, the town came alive with the sound of music and celebration. When Lord Stanley and his official party emerged, a 19-gun salute roared from the cannons of the Sydney Field Battery. Church bells rang and the

Sydney Coronet Band played. There was a parade through the town to the Court House on Charlotte Street for more ceremonies. The celebrations continued into the night.

On the Brink of Prosperity?

The completion of the rail line, marking as it did a tangible, land-based link between Cape Breton and the rest of North America, was taken by many to mean that the island had a great future. The *Cape Breton Handbook and Tourist Guide* of 1890 extolled the virtues of the island, describing its towns, villages and countryside in glowing terms. By virtue of its geography, mineral wealth and proximity to world markets, the author speculated, Cape Breton was on the brink of prosperity. The arrival of the ICR 'Iron Horse' was cited as an indication that change was in the air.

Such comments were of course the 'standard stuff' of tourist publications. In this instance, the writer himself might have been astonished at how accurate his prophesy of rapid change would prove.

For indeed, the elements were all in place. A catalyst was all that was needed to make it happen. That catalyst came to Cape Breton in 1893, in the form of an American syndicate headed by Boston industrialist, Henry Melville Whitney.

CHAPTER FIVE

The S&L Arrives, It's 1895

Strong ties between New England and Cape Breton date back centuries. New England ships fished and traded in Cape Breton waters since at least the early 1700s. Even during the French regime, when such contacts were discouraged by both sides, the relationship endured.

By the 19th century, American investment in the Cape Breton economy was commonplace. It had gone on for generations. Yet despite the longstanding practice, the project presented by H.M. Whitney in 1893 was something quite different. It was rare and unusual by any standards. Whitney was proposing a virtual takeover of the island's entire coal mining industry.

The Syndicate of H.M. Whitney

[Nature intended] that miners of Cape Breton should sell [coal] *in the New England market.*
— PREMIER W.S. FIELDING, quoting Sir Charles Tupper.

❖ ❖ ❖

The "Syndicate," or the "Whitney Syndicate" as it was sometimes called, got its start in the winter of 1891-92. Two Boston businessmen, Frederick Pearson and J.A. Grant purchased the Ontario Colliery at Glace Bay. Their construction firm had carried out a contract for Peoples' Heat and Light of Halifax in 1889. While in the provincial capital, they made a number of local business contacts which stirred their interest in Cape Breton mining. Pearson, a former instructor at the Massachusetts Institute of Technology, was also chief engineer at the West End Street Railway, a Massachusetts company owned by H.M. Whitney. How Whitney became actively involved in Cape Breton is not known for sure. Some say he was invited to make an investment with Pearson and Grant. Others claim individuals, like Sydney businessman Alexander Ross and Nova Scotia Premier W.S. Fielding made the first approach.

Whoever did the recruiting, the results were to change the face of one whole corner of Cape Breton Island. Whitney became enthusiastic about investing in the Cape Breton coal fields and put together a proposal that would revolutionize the industry. He began by assembling a group of American and Canadian investors to make a proposal to the Nova Scotia government. Premier Fielding supported the scheme almost from its inception.

After much negotiating, the parties made an agreement that included a 99-year lease over most of the island's coal reserves, a royalty rate fixed at 12½ cents per ton and a government subsidy to upgrade the railway system. Part of the upgrade was to build a new rail line to Louisbourg.

Fielding called the Nova Scotia House of Assembly into session in January 1893. After a brief debate, and over the protests of the opposition, the necessary legislation was passed. A few weeks later, on February 1, 1893, the Dominion Coal Company (DOMCO) was incorporated.

Dominion Coal

Within a year, Whitney and his associates acquired 70 square miles of coal leases. The area encompassed the properties of the Caledonia Coal and Railway Company; the International colliery of the International Coal Company; the Gardiner mine owned by the Burchell Brothers of Sydney; the Gowrie Coal Mining Company; the holdings of the Glace Bay Mining Company; Old Bridgeport owned by the International Coal Company; Reserve colliery of the Sydney and Louisburg Coal and Railway Company and the Victoria mines owned by David McKeen, M.P. of the Low Point, Barrasois and Lingan Mining Company. Only one major mine remained as an active, independent operation. It was part of the General Mining Association holdings, a group that was not included in the consolidation.

Dominion Coal moved quickly on a three-pronged approach to the modernization of the coal industry. Its focus was on the mines, on the ports (Sydney and Louisbourg), and on the railroads. The company shut down two mines, equipped the remaining six with modern machinery, and opened Dominion No.1 shaft on the Phalen coal seam. Huge new shipping piers, some of the largest in North America, were built at Sydney and in Louisbourg. Those in Sydney could accommodate six steamers at a time; in Louisbourg, three. The piers were

The coal and steel piers in Sydney. [S&LRHSoc.]

outfitted with their own electrical power generating systems allowing them to operate day and night. Some berths were reserved for bunkering to avoid delays for ships wanting fuel only.

The Black Diamond line, acquired from the International Coal and Railway Company during the consolidation, initially consisted of five steamers, two tugs and five barges. The fleet was supplemented by 27 steamships under charter. Their capacity ranged from 1500 to 6000 tons. Eventually 14 of the vessels were engaged in carrying coal to Montreal. In 1901, the company delivered 1,000,000 tons of coal to that port alone. The combined effect of the improvements was dramatic. Within a few years, production at Dominion Coal's mines had tripled to 3,000,000 tons a year.

Coal and Rail: The Political and Economic Background

Moving that amount of coal required an efficient railway system. In its original agreement with DOMCO, the provincial government devised a plan that they hoped would solve two problems at once.

For decades, there had been a sporadic political campaign to extend the Maritime's expanding railway system to Sydney and Louisbourg. It began as early as 1851 at a town meeting held in Sydney. Island politicians and town leaders lobbied the government to make the island the eastern terminus of the European and North American Railway.

The European and North American Railway was a railroad which was proposed for construction across New Brunswick and Nova Scotia. It was the brain child of John A. Poor, a promoter from Portland, Maine. In 1845 Poor persuaded Montreal investors to build a railway from Montreal to Portland. In 1850 he called a major convention in Portland to plan a further extension of that line across the hinterland of northern Maine, around the head of the Bay of Fundy through New Brunswick to Saint John and onward to Halifax.

Maine would build 222 miles of the proposed line, New Brunswick 204 and Nova Scotia 124. Once constructed, the line, in theory, would shorten the distance between Europe and the major centres along the Atlantic seaboard of North America.

In the end, however, it was an idea whose time had not come. Politicians in the Maritimes did not sign on to John A. Poor's "master plan." Instead, each area

DOMINION COAL CO. -FLEET LIST

Steamer Name	Built	Acquired	Disposition	Remarks
Tunstall	1879	1882	lost 1884	Purchased from J.S. Barwick
Coban	1882	1883	lost 1927	Purchased from Dent & Co.
Bonavista	1884	1886	lost 1912	Purchased from Babcock & Ratcliffe
Cacouna	1884	1886	lost 1914	Purchased from Babcock & Ratcliffe
Cape Breton	1890	?	lost 1920	
Louisburg (I)	1881	1892	lost 1918	Purchased from Geo. T. Davie, Levis
Corunna	1890	1913	sold ?	
Nevada	1890	1913	scrapped	
Cruizer (tug)	1895	1914	scrapped 1953?	Purchased from C.&C.G. Brister, Hfx
Heathcote	1898	1916	lost 1917	Purchased from H. McInnes, Hfx.
Rose Castle	1915	1921	lost 1942	
Lord Strathcona	1915	1920	lost 1942	
Wabana (I) renamed Canby	1911	1921	sold 1930 to Ropner & Co.	Went aground at Guyon Island, Cape Breton
Arthur Cross	1944	1946	sold 1965	
Wabana (II)	1943	1946	sold 1965	
Louisburg (II)	1943	1946	sold 1965	
Cibou	1932	1952	sold?	

built its own railroad piece by piece over the next decade and a half. In Nova Scotia, Joseph Howe was a strong advocate of public ownership of the railways. On the first round, he lost the debate, but he finally got his way when private investment bogged down in corruption and exorbitant maintenance costs. Completion of the system coincided with the big push for yet another railroad, the Intercolonial, as promised by Sir John A. Macdonald and other promoters of Canadian Confederation in 1867. The Intercolonial eventually absorbed much of the European and North American's rails in New Brunswick, along with the assets of the Nova Scotia Railway. An "all Canadian" route to Quebec was completed in 1876.

[As a new nation] Canada would become a major outlet for Cape Breton coal and that Louisburg would soon emerge as one of the greatest commercial cities of British North America.

—JOHN G. BOURINOT, 1866

❖ ❖ ❖

In Cape Breton, John G. Bourinot devoted much of his political career to the promotion of the Island's economic development, especially the coal trade and Sydney and Louisbourg harbours as shipping ports of major potential. In the pre-Confederation debates of 1866, as MLA and soon-to-be Senator, Bourinot spoke on the potential of Cape Breton coal and the importance of the projected Sydney and Louisburg railway.

Old ideas don't always go away. Once again in 1883, the federal government was petitioned to charter and subsidize the "Great American and European Short Line Railway Company." The focus of the petition was the construction of a National Trunk Air Line under one management, to run from Montreal through Maine, New Brunswick, and Nova Scotia, on to Cape Breton Island, and then over to the Colony of Newfoundland. [Despite the name "Air" Line, this was a proposal for train service.] With such a line, it was said, one would create "the shortest and safest transit to Europe." The promoters noted that sufficient data was not yet available concerning the Cape North and Newfoundland portions of the projected line. But rather than wait, they urged that a branch line be built to Sydney or Louisbourg, thereby forming a continuous route from Montreal to Louisbourg.

In 1890, a quarter century after the idea was first proposed, the Intercolonial Railway was finally extended to Sydney. With the development of the Dominion Coal Company, Premier Fielding and other politicians saw an opportunity, through the facilities of a private corporation, to link Louisbourg to the national rail system. It was a partial fulfilment of a commitment made so often, by so many politicians, over so many years.

The agreement the government signed with Dominion Coal granted a $3,200 per mile subsidy for the construction of a railroad between Bridgeport and Louisbourg. Further concessions include help in securing critical rights-of-way and land titles. There were, nonetheless, some restrictions imposed on the new corporate giant. The contract stipulated that after the survey, the distance of the new roadway would not exceed 28 miles. Construction was to include bridges, buildings, culverts, stations, station houses and all other works deemed necessary for the operation of a safe and efficient railroad. Furthermore, if construction was not completed on or before August 1, 1896, Dominion Coal would forfeit the subsidy. Another clause required the company to operate at least one passenger train each way daily except on Sunday.

Sorting Out the Lines

When it came time to survey the new line, the company found that a good part of the work had already been done. In the process of consolidating the various mining companies, the Whitney syndicate acquired a number of high profile employees. Among them: David McKeen, M.P., and John S. McLennan. Both men would later be named to the Senate. They joined Dominion Coal's first board of directors, McKeen as resident manager and McLennan as treasurer and company representative in Boston. McLennan, in a previous career as manager of the International Coal and Railway Company, had anticipated the need for a rail line to the winter port of Louisbourg. He had commissioned a survey of a new route between the coastal community and the long-established railroad at Bridgeport. When the Dominion Coal survey was complete, it followed closely the course laid out several years earlier. One major change, however, was to bring the line nearer the mines at Glace Bay and Cow Bay.

Hiram Donkin was the Dominion Coal Company's choice to head the project of consolidating the hodgepodge of tracks it had inherited. The consolidation involved a mixture of standard and narrow gauge lines. The standard gauge railways included the International Coal Company's 12 miles of track to their piers at Sydney harbour, a half mile branch to Old Bridgeport, and a mile and a half link with the Intercolonial Railway at Sydney. The railway of the New Victoria mines ran five miles to a pier at Sydney harbour. Then there was a one mile track from Caledonia mines and a half mile line from the Glace Bay mines, both ending at shipping piers in Glace Bay.

There were two narrow gauge lines: a railway of one and three quarter miles between Gowrie Mines and the company's loading pier at Cow Bay. And most notably, the Sydney and Louisburg railway of 34 miles in length between Sydney and Louisbourg with a 10-mile

The loading pier in Cow Bay (Morien). This postcard photo shows the bucket system taking coal to the pier - a slow system compounded by problems with ice in water [S&LRHSoc.]

branch line to Schooner Pond. The portion of the S&L running between the Reserve mines, Schooner Pond and Louisbourg had been defunct since 1883.

These ragtag railways were upgraded by Hiram Donkin. He brought them together in a rational system that was designed to serve the entire area more efficiently. He added a third rail to the old S&L/Gisborne line from Reserve to Sydney harbour. This enabled Dominion Coal to use both the standard and narrow gauge rolling stock they had inherited as part of the assets of the different coal companies cobbled together at the time of consolidation. For safety reasons, the two types of equipment were rarely mixed in one train.

Over time, all the narrow gauge running gear was weeded out of the system and standard gauge equipment became the norm. In 1902, most of the narrow gauge line to Sydney was turned over to Stone and Webster, a giant U.S.-based company with a network of street car operations throughout North America. They called the local tramway the Cape Breton Electric Company and ran the system between Sydney and Glace Bay and in the surrounding area. The company also offered a ferry service from Sydney to Westmount and to North Sydney, where passengers could make connections with a tramway to Sydney Mines. Both systems were discontinued in 1946.

Work on the extension from Bridgeport to Louisbourg began almost immediately after Dominion Coal was incorporated in 1893. The newly surveyed route brought the road bed closer to the coastline than the old Gisborne road had done. This was to reach new coal seams the company hoped to exploit in the Glace Bay and Cow Bay basin. Like every railroad building project, much attention was given to grades and elevations. One consideration was that most of the freight would be coal and travelling in one direction, towards Louisbourg. With that in mind, Hiram Donkin was careful to choose the most advantageous trail. The result was a 27-mile route that conformed in every way to the government's contract requirements. The roadway was determined to be on a par with the government's own rail line, the recently completed Intercolonial Railway.

In a paper read before the Mining Society of Nova Scotia in 1894, Hiram Donkin paid tribute to the beautiful scenery around Mira Bay and Catalone Lake calling it "unsurpassed in this country." He concluded that "as for historic Louisbourg — the Atlantic terminus of the line — . . . under modern conditions, though on different lines, [it] is certainly destined to resume something at least of its former glory."

Historic Ceremony, 1895

Whilst the railway from Sydney to Louisburg is essentially a railway for the cheap transportation of coal, and has been located solely with that object in view, it will not be without interest to the travelling public.

— HIRAM DONKIN, 1894

❖ ❖ ❖

By happy coincidence, the completion of the S&L railroad to Louisbourg in 1895 coincided with a significant date in the town's distant past, the 150th anniversary of the siege of 1745. The two events, present and past, were linked by a memorial staged in Louisbourg. It was sponsored by the Society of Colonial Wars, a historical group based in the United States. That organization was dedicated to marking major events in pre-revolutionary American history. One of the first projects was to erect a granite column at Louisbourg as a monument to the New England siege of 1745.

The announcement of the plan was greeted with mixed reviews in Canada. Some saw it in a positive light. Others did not. Three French-language newspapers were joined by the *Antigonish Casket* and the United Empire Loyalists Association of Canada in voicing a strong protest. Each, for perhaps differing reasons, took exception to the idea of a group from a foreign country raising a memorial on Canadian soil to commemorate a battle that was essentially a Canadian defeat. The *Antigonish Casket* called it an insult. New Brunswick Senator Pascal Poirier added his own objections with a speech in the Senate stating that the proposed monument "aroused an unpleasant feeling" in the Maritimes and violated the norms of "international decency". Prime Minister Sir Mackenzie Bowell sidestepped Poirier's pointed remarks, claiming the government knew little about the matter as it was being undertaken by a private organization on private land. The ceremony went ahead as planned, on 17 June 1895.

Despite the protests, the Louisbourg event was the culmination of a four-day gala celebration. It began on June 14 when the Nova Scotia Historical Society hosted the Society of Colonial Wars at the Council Chamber of the Provincial Building in Halifax. On Saturday both groups travelled by private train coach to Sydney as guests of Sir Malachy Daly, Lieutenant-Governor of Nova Scotia. Daly was standing in for the Governor-General, the Earl of Aberdeen, who sent his regrets. Sunday was spent in Sydney and on Monday morning, June 17, the Dominion Coal Company assembled two trains to carry the official party and the public along its newly completed railroad for an inaugural trip to Louisbourg. In all, 1200 people rode the two trains. An equal number travelled to Louisbourg by other means.

The first train arrived in Louisbourg at 11 AM. It carried Lt-Gov. Daly, the Colonial Wars Committee, the Sydney committee and their guests. Louisbourg's main street was decorated for the occasion with flags and bunting. The warship HMS *Canada* and the Dominion cruiser *Curlew* were at anchor in the harbour, decked out in similar fashion. Even visiting merchant vessels displayed their colours for the occasion. The dignitaries were taken on board the *Canada* for a brief visit. Other members of the party travelled from the station by horse and carriage past the ruins of the Grand (Royal) Battery and on to the site of the Fortress. As Lt-Gov. Daly left the *Canada* on the ship's tender, he was honoured with a military salute of 11 guns. Arriving at the beach below the Fortress shortly after noon, Daly, the U.S. visitors and other dignitaries were escorted to a large tent for a luncheon hosted by the local committee. The proceedings were delayed for a time to allow the huge crowd to assemble on the grounds of the Fortress. In due course, a parade was formed. Led by 25 members of the Sydney Brass Band, the procession marched to the ruins of the King's Bastion, which was the site of the unveiling.

Society members and dignitaries pose beneath the granite column of the Pepperell monument at Fortress Louisbourg. Bottom row from left: Capt. W.W. Lewis, Rev. T.F. Draper, Warden Henry LeVatte, Edward McAlpine, Jim MacPhee (owned the Presbyterian Church when it was a store).
[S&LRHSoc.]

An estimated 2500 people attended the festivities, which included two hours of speeches by luminaries from Canada and the United States. The invocations, prayers and several of the presentations struck a high tone that reflected the solemnity of the occasion. Others were tinged with a more jingoistic flavour.

In late afternoon, Lt-Gov. Daly unveiled the granite monument on a level plane near the King's Bastion. It was a column of Roman Tuscan design, 26 feet high, and situated on a prominent position on high ground, visible for miles around. The inscription on four sides read: "To commemorate the capture of Louisbourg A.D. 1745. Erected by the Society of Colonial Wars A.D. 1895. 'Provincial Forces' Massachusetts Bay, Connecticut, New Hampshire 4,000 men under Lieutenant-General Pepperrell. 'British Fleet' 10 sail, 500 guns under Commodore Warren. 'Provincial Fleet' 16 Armed Vessels, 19 transports, 240 Guns under Captain Tyng. To Our Heroic Dead, 'French Forces' 2,500 regulars Militia and Seamen under Governor Duchambon."

Rev. T.F. Draper, Rector of St. Bartholomew's Anglican Church in Louisbourg, pronounced the benediction. The Sydney brass band played God Save the Queen and an honour guard of bluejackets and marines from HMS *Canada* presented arms. The procession formed, led by the *Canada's* fife and drum corps which played American airs. It wended its way to the shore where the guests on the invitation of Captain Wilson, boarded the ship's tender. They were taken on board the warship for refreshments. After an hour's entertainment, the group returned to the waiting train for the return trip to Sydney. In the city there were closing ceremonies at the parlour rooms of the Sydney Hotel, a final round of speeches and a chorus of "Auld Lang Syne" to close out the day. The next morning, June 18, the members of the Colonial Wars Society and other dignitaries returned to their special cars at the Sydney train station for the homeward journey. The train left Sydney at 5 AM and arrived in Halifax at 6 PM.

On the last leg of their "progress" across the province, the party stopped in New Glasgow for dinner. There the Hotel Vendome presented the following menu to honour the occasion: Colonial Soup; Salmon à la Warren; Tongue Aix-la-Chapelle; Acadian Spring Lamb; Roast Beef John Bull, with Pepperrell Sauce; French Pickles; Gabarus Potatoes; Pomeroy Peas; New England Pumpkin Pie; Louisbourg Pudding; Strawberries, Isle Royale. "NIL DESPERANDUM CHRISTO DUCE."

Local committee members from Sydney had included A.J. McDonald, Mayor of Sydney; Kenneth McKinnon; Joseph H. Hearn, Recorder and Secretary; Angus G. McLean. From Louisbourg there was H.C.V. LeVatte; Chairman Wm. W. Lewis; Rev. T. Fraser Draper; Roderick McDonald; Neil J. Townsend; Charles R. Mitchell; James McPhee, Treasurer; and Edward S. McAlpine, Secretary.

The Sydney and Louisburg Railway was launched on a high note full of pomp and circumstance. It would be hard to match again in the workaday life of a commercial rail line.

> *The arrangements for the celebration were practically perfect and were carried out without a hitch. Not a mishap of any kind occurred to mar the pleasure of the day's proceedings, although the gathering was the largest Louisburg has witnessed in modern times. Everybody left the grounds, the scene of bloody conflict one hundred and fifty years ago, feeling that the people of Canada and the United States were nearer together than ever before and mentally vowing that, if they could prevent it, neither England nor the United States nor England and France should ever again meet in bloody strife on the battlefield. Canada, as the representative of Great Britain, clasped hands in friendship with the United States across the bloody chasms of 1776 and 1812, and both extended the olive branch of peace and fraternity to brave and chivalrous France and her warm-hearted sons on this continent; and so auspiciously the third capture of Louisburg, by the combined American and Canadian forces, on June 17, 1895, ended.*
>
> — Comments in the Halifax paper, THE MORNING CHRONICLE, 18 June 1895

CHAPTER SIX

The S&L Line And Its Heyday

The old Gisborne railroad, especially the Reserve to Louisbourg section, was dotted with trestles, bridges and culverts made of wood. This was typical of early roadbuilding where the motivating factor was getting things up and running and producing revenue as soon as possible. Later, as time and money allowed, developers would go back and upgrade the parts that needed to be replaced with concrete and steel. The Louisbourg end of the Gisborne line, with its short lifespan, never reached that complete stage of development.

The 1895 version of the Sydney & Louisburg Railway differed greatly from its predecessor. From the roadbed up, the S&L was built and equipped in a manner that suggested permanence. The most notable part of the line — from many a perspective — was the 34-mile stretch between Sydney and Louisbourg, with a 10-mile branch to Schooner Pond. The portion of the S&L running between the Reserve Mines, Schooner Pond and Louisbourg had been defunct since 1883.

Details of the S&L Line

Charts for the first Sydney to Louisbourg survey followed a route that conformed closely to the specifications set out by the company and the government. This proposed to bring the railroad across the valley of the Catalone Brook requiring a structure of nearly a mile in length and at an average height of 70 feet. The estimated cost was astronomical, so an alternate route was found. The grade would be steeper, but even with the use of an auxiliary engine factored into the equation, the new route was considered cost effective.

When the railway was completed, Hiram Donkin had achieved what both the government

The Louisbourg Station about 1910. Note the shingled freight shed walls which had originally been built with a board-and-batten finish. There is also a pile of telegraph poles behind the shed. [S&LRHSoc.]

Waiting for the train to arrive in Louisburg in 1901. As in most small communities, the Louisbourg Station was the center of much activity during arrivals and departures. [S&LRHSoc.]

and the company had requested. The new route from Sydney to Louisbourg was 37 miles long and came within striking distance of most mining areas in the Cow Bay and Glace Bay basins. There were several major structures erected along the line. At Little Glace Bay Brook, Big Glace Bay Brook and Black Brook there were steel trestles of 150 feet each and 25 to 30 feet high. Meanwhile, the Mira River Bridge required three spans of steel and iron of 100 feet each. At the outlet of Catalone Lake there was a span of 50 feet; while a steel trestle was put up at the crossing of Catalone Lake and the Summit, 360 feet in length and averaging 50 feet in height.

The roadbed required 3000 cubic yards of ballast per mile and 7000 cubic yards of masonry to insure proper drainage and passage of streams. The steel rails were 80 lbs. per lineal yard and they were supported on cedar ties laid every two feet. Joint fastenings were the most modern available and steel "Servis" tie plates were used throughout the entire length of the line. Almost 600,000 cubic yards of material, mostly rock, had to be removed to clear the right-of-way which measured 22 feet in cuttings and 16 feet on embankments.

Many buildings along the S&L line were built in the "railroad" style of the day. With steeply-pitched roofs, dormers and gable ends; clapboard siding and wide overhanging eaves skirting all four sides of the buildings, they bore many characteristics of railroad architecture as seen throughout Canada at the turn-of-the century. Usually located near the center of town as was the case in Glace Bay and Louisbourg, they were among the most prominent structures in most small communities. Only a few examples remain today. They include the restored station house and freight shed at Louisbourg, the only "survivors" of the S&L line.

The Coal Pier at Louisbourg

The completion of the S&L Line to Louisbourg, along with the construction of a coal pier, meant that Louisbourg had finally come to play the role envisioned for the port by Gisborne, Kennelly and others. Almost immediately, the town acquired a new identity.
Turn-of-the-century newspapers began calling Louisbourg the *Winter Port*, and the *Ice-free Port*. Readers throughout Cape Breton knew those terms described Louisbourg.

The S&L track that came into Louisbourg came past the S&L station and along what is now Huntington Avenue. It crossed Main Street and ended at a newly-constructed pier that

These small boats would be loaded down to within a few inches of the water line. You'd think they'd be sunk getting out of the harbour. The pumps would be going! I remember talking to one captain, he was putting bags of coal on the deck. He said — "Whatever I put on the deck there — that's clear profit. I make a lot of money with that. If the pumps start going, I just throw some bags overboard." I wish I had some pictures of them. The thought of it still makes me shudder but it didn't bother them. Second nature to them I guess.

—JOHN O'NEILL, longtime trainman with the S&L

❖ ❖ ❖

Carpenters posing on the Louisburg Pier. Note that the buildings covering the conveyor belt overhead have not been completed.
Front Row (left to right): Jack Townsend, Alf. Baldwin, Norman MacLeod, Charlie Dickson, Phil Townsend, Dannie MacPherson, Tom Cann. Second Row (left to right): W. Baldwin, Morris Kehoe, Harry Townsend, Christopher Morrison, Harry Ley, Judson Cross, John MacMullin, Billie Wilcox, Neil McDonald, Roddie NcNeil, Sandy Johnson, Jack Ransome.
[S&LRHSoc.]

extended into the harbour. The pier was 600 feet long, 90 feet wide and the approach was along a trestle 450 feet in length. Coal trains stopped at the pier entrance and the engine was separated and diverted to a lower track for watering and bunkering. There they awaited the empty coal cars. Brakemen disconnected the caboose and the line of hopper cars rolled out onto the pier where each car in turn was uncoupled and its bottom doors were opened and its cargo dumped down a chute and into the hold of a ship or barge waiting at dockside. A drop-table then delivered the hopper car to a lower track where it rolled by gravity to a marshalling area and the waiting locomotive. When all the cars were empty, the train was reassembled and the caboose reattached and off it would go, back to the mine site for another load. The Dominion Coal Company had upgraded the old International piers in Sydney in a similar manner but on a larger scale.

To speed up the loading process and to ensure that there was always a good supply of coal on hand, Dominion Coal added a large capacity coal pocket to its Louisbourg operations in 1901. A conveyor belt system was developed to deliver coal directly from the pocket along the pier and into the ship's hold. In combination with the coal trains unloading directly from the pier, this additional technology increased the port's capacity. Rapid loading and turn around time, critical aspects of the shipping industry, were greatly improved.

To service the piers, the company installed a boiler house and electrical plant. It provided power for the conveyor system and electric lights on the pier and along the harbour to the S&L station. The Town of Louisbourg did not get electrical service until around 1916 which meant that the lights along the waterfront from the 1902-3 period were a novelty.

Most of the coal carried by the S&L to Louisbourg was destined for large ships bound for ports all over the world. It made the community an exciting place. Rose O'Keefe O'Neill, who was born in Louisbourg in 1907, recalls how people would scan the horizon each day, hoping for the first

> *One step through that gate and you are in a steam fan's paradise. Around you are locomotives of various sizes and types, open-platform wooden passenger cars, curious long box cars with high windows and rough seats for carrying miners to the pits, and dismounted tenders turned on side to save space. There is even a jumbo crane that helped to build the almost-legendary Chignecto Ship Railway 85 years ago and is still working. You are in the midst of all the interesting, nostalgic stuff that an engine terminal has accumulated in nearly a century of steam railroading. Coal rumbles down chutes, firemen manipulate tank spouts on tender tops, smoke drifts lazily from a dozen stacks, turntables rumble, and iron horses chuff in and out, amid the oldtime mixed smells of hot oil, exhaust steam, and burning soft coal.*
>
> *— H.B. Jefferson, 1960*

This excellent view of the Louisbourg Piers shows the freight pier (left) and the coal pier (right). The small shed next to the hoppers on the coal pier is the scale house to weigh the coal cars. Note the CN boxcars in the foreground. The S&L handled much of the CN's freight. [S&LRHSoc.]

glimpse of approaching ships. Their arrival caused a "commotion," and meant welcome "work for the men of the town."

While large ships carried away most of the coal, there was a significant demand for coal by small boats as well. Fishing boats from Newfoundland, called "jacks", came frequently to Louisbourg, especially in the fall of year. They would take the coal and deliver it to outports along the Newfoundland coast.

The Dominion Coal Company established a fire department at the pier in 1905. (The Town of Louisbourg did not mount a campaign for a volunteer crew until 1928.) This was a necessary step because the coal pocket caught fire with unfortunate regularity. Throughout the coal industry, fires and explosions were a constant hazard.

A second wharf was built at Louisbourg to the east of the coal pier. It was used for handling freight and later for shipping steel from the Sydney steel plant. For many years the Newfoundland ferries called at the winter port of Louisbourg, so that the freight pier became a landing area for passengers coming or going on the S&L line. In addition to the port facilities, the Louisbourg division of the S&L included a station house, freight shed, a two-bay engine shed and a marshalling yard. The company built a turntable in Louisbourg but rarely used it, so the engines had to make the return trip to Sydney in reverse. The Sydney terminus of the line had a rail loop which allowed the engine to turn about, but Glace Bay was the only location with a true turntable. Fortunately, the mechanics of a steam engine allows it to run with equal efficiency in forward or reverse. The only concession necessitated by this forward-backward running was that several of the engines had to have the coal tenders modified to improve the engineers' view when travelling in reverse.

Glace Bay: The Hub

Glace Bay became the unquestioned hub of the S&L rail network. H.B. Jefferson, a writer for *Railway Magazine* described a visit to the Glace Bay operation in a 1960 article entitled "100 Percent Steam". He was enthralled by the "time capsule" he discovered when he turned off Reserve Road and entered the S&L compound, a place that was regarded with reverence by many enthusiasts of the age of steam locomotion.

Engine 105 in an engine shed. Note the stacks on the roof of the building to allow the engines to keep their fires up inside. [S&LRHSoc.]

The Glace Bay roundhouse, as its name implies, was originally circular in shape. Over time, it was enlarged as it evolved into a combination roundhouse and engine shed. Its final shape resembled a giant irregular horseshoe with the turntable at the heel end.

Throughout the year, the S&L locomotives were brought to the Glace Bay compound for any needed repairs. During the miners' summer holiday, when the collieries were virtually idle, most of the engines were concentrated at the "Bay". The foundry, machine shop and car shop were just north of the Bay roundhouse. Nearby was a 20,000-gallon water tank with its distinctive coolie-hat, wood-shingled top and a bunkering station where fuel was discharged by one-ton box loads into locomotive tenders. Closer to the centre of town was the

Photo taken from the turntable showing the engine stalls of the Roundhouse, Glace Bay. [S&LRHSoc.]

Glace Bay Yard. View looks towards Glace Bay Station. Large building at left is the forge. [S&LRHSoc.]

Glace Bay station and general office, the communications and administrative centre of the entire operation.

Any piece of rolling stock that was damaged was taken back to the shops at Glace Bay where all routine maintenance or emergency repair was carried out. The company developed a skilled workforce of mechanics that could handle any type of repair that might be needed. By the 1950s, crews had rebuilt scores of locomotives, sometimes fabricating parts that were no longer available. Superintendent of motive power, Joseph G. Fisher, a veteran employee of the S&L who headed up the mechanical division for years, enjoyed an impressive reputation as an authority on steam locomotives. Dozens of Cape Bretoners learned their trade at the Glace Bay compound of the S&L and became highly qualified mechanics.

The section man's trailer is in the foreground, and the short lengths of rail used to remove it from the tracks at Victoria Junction. [S&LRHSoc.]

Beyond Glace Bay, 11 miles to the west, was Victoria Junction. There, most trains and engines received their terminal clearance. A 7-mile spur line was built from there to New Waterford (Barrachois Cove) when the company opened Dominion No. 12 colliery around 1908. More spur lines were added over the years as new mining areas opened up. A mile and a half further west of Victoria Junction was the main assembly or marshalling yards. One mile beyond was Sydney Junction where lines radiated out to the Sydney engine terminal, the Intercolonial/Canadian National yards, the Sydney steel plant and the International piers. The loading piers at Sydney were a larger scale version of the ones located at Louisbourg. An average of 10 engines worked the Sydney end of the line.

Train Wreck at Mira, 1903

Can a shipwreck cause a trainwreck? It would seem so. The S&L Railway found out how in 1903.

On Tuesday afternoon, April 14, 1903, Lou Petrie was preparing the steamer *Alameda* of the Mira River service for a short sail to Scatarie Island, not far from Louisbourg. The

Amnity, a sailing barque, had gone ashore on the island and Petrie was taking her master, a Captain Olsen, to inspect the wrecked vessel. Captain Neilson of the steamer *Britannic* and Captain Cann of the *E.M. Cates* were going along to assist. All was in readiness and Mira River bridge attendant James McDonald opened the draw about three quarters of the way to allow the *Alameda* to exit into Mira Bay. Captain Petrie, about to cast off the lines, had been doing some last minute negotiations with a local man by the name of Phillips, a certified engineer. He was hoping Phillips would join the salvage team as a crew member.

While the above discussions were going on, S&L Engine No. 62 was travelling west bound from Louisbourg with a long train of empty coal cars. It was crewed by Charles J. MacDonald, conductor, James Parsons, engineer, Charles Dickson, fireman, George Wadden, head brakeman and Harold Cann, end brakeman. The powerful locomotive was under a full head of steam as it emerged from a rock cut and rounded a curve on its approach to the Mira River.

Engineer Parsons and fireman Dickson, from their vantage point high in the cab, could see the open section of the draw bridge and immediately made frantic efforts to stop the train. Unlike today's rolling stock with air brakes and extra assists, safety devices were few and far between in the early 20th century. Parsons blew the whistle for extra brakes, threw the locomotive into reverse, and applied sand to the drive wheels. By the time the train entered the first span, it had slowed to a speed of about four miles an hour. Nonetheless it was apparent that a disaster was unavoidable.

When the train was about half way across the bridge and the pony wheels of the engine were just going over the abutment, fireman Dickson leaped from the cab and clung to a girder. The engine plunged into the icy water, about 25 feet deep at mid-stream. The cab broke off and crashed into the river. Three empty cars followed in quick succession.

The conductor and brakeman, who were travelling further back in the train, ran to the river bank. A small dory was launched from the *Alameda* in an attempt to rescue James Parsons. Crew members Angus McDonald and Ignatius Campbell quickly recovered his body floating nearby, but efforts to revive him failed. Dr. McKeen arrived shortly thereafter and determined that he had been killed instantly by the impact. A veteran railroader, well liked by his fellow trainmen, Parsons had joined the S&L about a year earlier after a career with the Grand Trunk railway.

Engine 62, nose down in the Mira River. [H.O. Dodge]

Strong tidal currents and the enormous weight of the equipment made cleaning up the wreck a tough job. In charge were C.S. Clayton and John Leaman, who at that time was fire chief in Glace Bay. With the help of divers, they turned the engine over in the river and built a temporary railroad underneath. Locomotive No. 62 was hauled ashore and onto the main line. It was removed to Glace Bay, rebuilt, and returned to the S&L Line for another 25 years service.

Surviving crew members of that ill-fated train went on to other things. Conductor Charles J. MacDonald eventually became Secretary of Labour for Nova Scotia. George Wadden was

I was the only young fellow on the section. They were all older men. They were all hard workers and you had to keep up with them. There were ten section gangs at that time. I was on section #1 at the Pier. We had about 13 miles of track to look after. Our section started at the Pier round house to the coke ovens. Then from the coke ovens down to Sydney Branch to the CNR trestle. We also had the Sydney Coal Yard and the coal bank which was at the coke ovens — known as Mullin's Bank. There were 6 men on each section at the time I started.

— IVAN BATES, who began working for the S&L during World War II, at the age of 15. All young men over 18 had been called up to serve in the armed forces. Thus Mr. Bates was the only young fellow on the crew.

❖ ❖ ❖

A diver stands on the barge, while another worker stands on the boiler of the now completely submerged locomotive. [S&LRHSoc.]

promoted to become S&L conductor at Sydney. Harry Cann, who survived the Mira wreck, was later killed in a railroad accident at Morien Junction. Charles Dickson, the fireman who jumped to safety seconds before the crash, was interviewed by the Sydney *Post Record* in April 1933, on the 30th anniversary of the fatal accident. He recalled the events vividly and noted that to his knowledge, the draw bridge had not been opened for years before that fateful afternoon in April 1903.

The Crews

Maintaining the roadbed and track was a never-ending job. For the purpose of repair and upkeep, the S&L, like every other railway of any size, was divided into sections. Originally,

Engine 59 lies on her side in a wreck, August 16, 1920, red Bridge, Dominion, N.S. [S&LRHSoc.]

there were 18 sections. Over time that number diminished to five. Each section had a foreman and a crew of five men on average, to make sure the rails were kept in good condition. Each group followed a routine that involved a daily inspection of the entire track to see that everything, rails, roadbed and switches were in good order.

In the early days, inspections were done from a pumpcar with its seesaw handles, familiar as a favourite prop in silent movies. Later, a gas-powered motorcar or "speedy" replaced the muscle power of the pumpcar. More recently, a truck with retractable steel wheels is used to bring men and materials to the work site. Ditching the roadbed to maintain proper drainage, replacing culverts, renewing wooden ties and stone ballast and a hundred other routine tasks were done on a priority basis. But those routines were put aside when an emergency arose: a derailment or a run-off, a washout or a heavy snowstorm.

Crews were on 24-hour call. If the task was too big for one crew, men from other sections

We'd be out day and night trying to keep roads open for trains going to the collieries and coal yards; Seaboard, the wash plant, Nova Scotia Power Plant with plough and flanger. Engines getting stuck in snow banks. Some of the worse places we had to look after were Sydney hill; they called it the Banjo and another place was Old Victoria . . . Snow blowing off the lake. It was really bad there. Sometimes there would be drifts 15 feet high at Old Victoria. I've seen engines getting stuck on the Banjo and we would have to shovel it out. They would get some of the men from the coal piers in Sydney to help shovel the engines out. It was pretty tough going.

— IVAN BATES, who worked for the S&L for 44 years, recalling winter snow storms on the line.

❖ ❖ ❖

were called in to help. Veterans of the S&L can recall many occasions when getting the trains rolling again took an all out effort lasting three or four 24-hour shifts. Snowstorms could be, as one veteran railroader put it, "pretty tough going."

Another painstaking job was that of righting engines and railcars that had gone off the tracks. Getting them back on the tracks took skill and patience. In the early days much of the effort was "bull work" with fairly rustic equipment. The track was straightened or realigned by gangs of men with steel pry bars. Spikes were driven in the classic style by two men swinging their sledge hammers in perfect syncopation, tapping out a beat that was once as much the rhythm of the railroad as the clickty-clack of the steel wheels. Today, much of that work is done by a motorized spiking machine.

Early railroaders were innovative in using what they had to get a job done. Often they called in a second engine to nudge a derailed locomotive back onto the tracks. Like a beached whale, the mighty machine was prodded and poked; wedges placed under its wheels until it was manoeuvred, inch by painstaking inch, back onto the track. It was dangerous, frustrating work where one slip could prove disastrous, even deadly.

Especially in winter, the task of calling the crews out to work was sometimes easier said than done. Longtime S&L engineer Lauchie MacDonald remembers how as a youth he had been a "call boy" for the railway. This meant he had to trek through the Whitney Pier district calling out a train crew. This had to be done on snowshoes on occasion. The company rule was that employee seniority lists were posted on a "call board," and when a supervisor was making up a crew from that list he would send out the "call boy" to contact each employee.

The Mechanics' Trade

The mechanics' trade had a long tradition in Cape Breton, an area which had known railroading, in one form or another, from the 1830s and 1840s when coal tramways were in use at Bridgeport and in Sydney Mines. As the technology advanced, so did the abilities of the men using the machines. In 1886, for example, the men of the General Mining Association's foundry and shops at Sydney Mines were given the assignment to build a locomotive.

The mechanics' tradition continues at the Cape Breton Development Corporation's "Devco" Railway, the successor to the S&L operation.

THE "C.G. SWANN"

In 1886, the men of the General Mining Association's foundry and shops at Sydney Mines were given a special assignment. They were asked to build a locomotive. Chief Engineer John Elliot and his crew of pattern makers, moulders, blacksmiths, machinists and fitters replicated a machine already in service with the company. They named it the "C.G. Swann" after an official of the Association. A unique achievement, it is thought to be the only steam locomotive ever built on the island. After a trial run, it was floated on a barge across Sydney Harbour to South Bar and used on the Victoria Mines Railroad for many years.

— FRED CALDER, July 7, 1974

Photographed with their impressive creation are: In the cab, Chief Engineer John Elliot. From left to right: Foreman pattern maker James MacDonald, moulder foreman Richard Partridge, machinist John Wilson, machinist John M. MacDonald, fitter Robert Bonner Sr., foreman blacksmith Joseph Howetson, machinist Robert Bonner Jr. and moulder Alfred J. Gregg. *[S&LRHSoc.]*

On June 10, 1983, Devco opened its new Rail Center at Victoria Junction. It is an ultra modern version of the old Glace Bay shops it replaced. Work areas are clean, brightly lit and well ventilated. Nostalgia for the days of steam, even among veteran railway buffs, does not often include the smoke and ashes, the down side of coal-fired locomotives. The new facility has the men and machinery needed to keep the company's fleet of hopper cars and diesel electric locomotives running smoothly. They also do repair work for the new Cape Breton and Central Nova Scotia Railway, now operated by RailTex, a holding company based in San Antonio, Texas. Some of Devco's employees are second and third generation railway men, their grandfathers having worked on the S&L line.

The Norris Family
From left to right:
Ralph, Gerald, J.J.(Jack),
Graham and Lawrence Norris.

The Norris Family

The Norris Family has the distinction of having five members of their family who worked for the S&L railroad. To the best of their knowledge, this may be a first for the S&L railroad to have that many members of one family working for the company.

The sons were all born in Glace Bay and moved to the Morien Station area in 1935, with their parents John and Glady's (nee Welch) Norris. Also, there were five sisters, Margaret, Eunice, Evelyn, Mae and Barbara.

John Joseph (Jack) Norris, who was their father, started with the S&L Railroad in 1908 and was in the brotherhood of railroad trainmen for 50 years. Jack was a conductor on the trains which took the coal miners from Morien and Birch Grove, to the coal colleries of Glace Bay. He then would go to his job as a conductor at #2 and #20 colleries on the shunter.

Ralph Norris, who was the oldest son and brother, started working on the steam locomotives in the round house, tempering locomotive springs, and then he became a car inspector in Sydney.

Lawrence Norris was hired as a brakeman, after coming out of the Air Force (World War II). Later on he became a conductor.

Gerald Norris worked on the section branch from Morien to Mira.

Graham Norris, the youngest brother, worked as a car inspector at the Caledonia Junction.

The S&L itself, of course, often contained a couple of generations of different families. The Norris family of Glace Bay (and later from Morien), for instance, sent first the father and then four sons to work for the S&L. They served variously as conductors, brakemen, blacksmiths, inspectors and sectionmen.

Many men who have made the transition from steam trains to diesel electric can remember a time when an engineer or fireman carried a tool kit with him on every train run as part of his basic equipment. If there was a breakdown, the train crew could often make do with an adjustment here or a patch there. Today in the age of diesel electric engines, most troubles have to be left to the experts. Trainmen have a checklist of proscribed procedures they run through. If that does not correct the problem, the train is shut down and a crew of expert mechanics is called out. The technology is greatly advanced with much of the circuitry now being run by computers.

Lingo

Railroading, like most trades, developed its own vocabulary over time. To the uninitiated, "shifting-links," "sliding blocks," "cross heads" and "equalizing beams" sound mysterious. To people who worked on a steam railway, however, such terms were a familiar part of the daily work routine.

One unusual expression was tractive-power. It meant the draw bar pulling power of the locomotive and was used to determine the machine's capacity to haul railcars and freight. A small device that resembled a circular slide rule was designed to simplify the calculation. Patented in New York in 1896, it was called a "Locomotive Tractive-Power Computer" and was probably the first "computer" ever used to help run a railroad.

Cletus Egan, of Glace Bay, for many years chief clerk of the S&L general office, has among his collection of railroad memorabilia, a small notebook in which he had noted tractive-power figures for many of the S&L locomotives. The calculations were made with the help of the "computer" and kept on hand for quick reference when trains were being assembled. Egan vividly recalls the time and effort involved in keeping track of the S&L rolling stock. By 1940, the company had 1,500 coal cars of its own and 500 more under lease, plus 26 locomotives. Knowing where all that equipment was at any given time was a challenge. Mr. Egan can recall

If a steam engine had any advantages over a diesel, and there weren't many — if anything went wrong with the steam engine, you actually had two engines; one on each side. It's just like two engines. You've got a piston and rods and wheels on each side and sometimes if a rod would come loose and get bent up, well they would take it off and take the main rod off and centre the valve on that side and block it there and take the engine home with the power from that side. Instead of having to be towed in, they would take her in on one side — just the power from one piston.

— HARVEY MACLEOD, who started with the S&L in 1948, when he was 17. At that time he worked seven days a week at 76 cents per hour. He retired in 1990 after 42 years of railway work.

❖ ❖ ❖

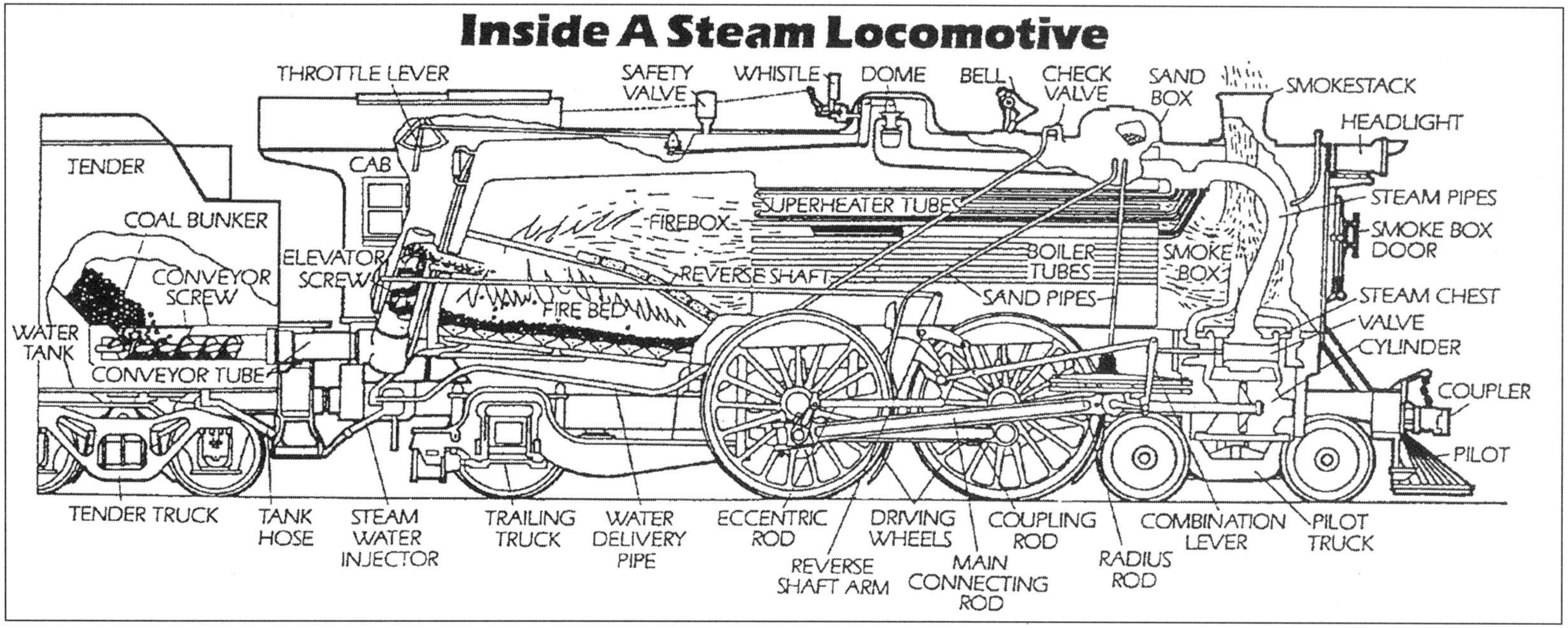

This cut-away diagram of a steam locomotive reveals the inner workings of the "Iron Horse." Note the elaborate system of conveyor screws and tubes involved in the automatic stoker. It delivered a steady supply of coal from the tender to the firebox. In the S&L fleet of 31 steam locomotives, only 7 were equipped with automatic stokers. The rest were hand fired. The diagram also reveals a network of sanding devices. During inclement weather or when the engine was labouring under a heavy load, a trickle of sand could be released to increase the traction between the drive wheels and the slick surface of the rail. Sanders are still vital to the operation of modern diesel trains.

(Reprinted from *Popular Mechanics*, May 1989. ©Copyright the Helpst Corporation. All Rights reserved.)

that at times, part of his job involved going out along the S&L network of spur lines and sidings, rounding up "strays," empty cars that had escaped from the recording system and bringing them back into the inventory.

As it was essential for each unit or section of the S&L to spend many long hours together — the same men might work together for decades — it was inevitable that working relationships among crew members came to resemble those of an extended family. Part of the relationship, and the routine, was that good-natured joking and teasing went on throughout the working day. Everyone had a nickname. Equally, everyone had a story to tell. Some railwaymen also liked to compose humourous verses to entertain their fellow workers. The poems below were composed by Archie MacVicar and Joe R. MacDonald, on the occasion of Mr. MacVicar's retirement from a lifetime around the tracks, first with the S&L and then with the DEVCO Railway. The "Donald Report" that is referred to is the report of a Royal Commission that recommended nationalizing the Cape Breton coal mines and the transfer of the S&L Railway to DEVCO.

Farewell

My last run for DEVCO I remember quite well,
Joe R he was driving and going like hell.
We had 202 the pretty and Red Van
And Alex-Nick was the CON-DUC-TOR MAN.

I felt a bit blue but didn't let on
We had Charlie Dickson, and we had Donald John,
When we started our work out, 'twas snowing quite hard.
The shop first said Angie and then the Coal Yard.

When you finish the Coal Yard, there's no time for soup:
O'Neil's has no empties, get a train off the loop.
Wherever I wander, and wherever I go,
I will always remember the High and the Low.

I gave up my turn and I'm done using sand,
I'm heading for Louisbourg, the best in the land.
I'm going on pension and happy for that
And I'm asking you Gillis, LOOK AFTER THAT CAT.

Now time is a-passing, I must end this rhyme;
The day's work is over, we're in just on time.
I gave my lunch can to Kenny, for myself kept the quart,
God bless you all and the DONALD REPORT.

ARCHIE MACVICAR, November 29, 1968

Response

No more stories, no more lies
For all that's left of us poor working guys.
We're going to miss you and miss you a lot
We'll see you at Christmas and I hope have a shot.

THE S&L BOYS, November 30, 1968

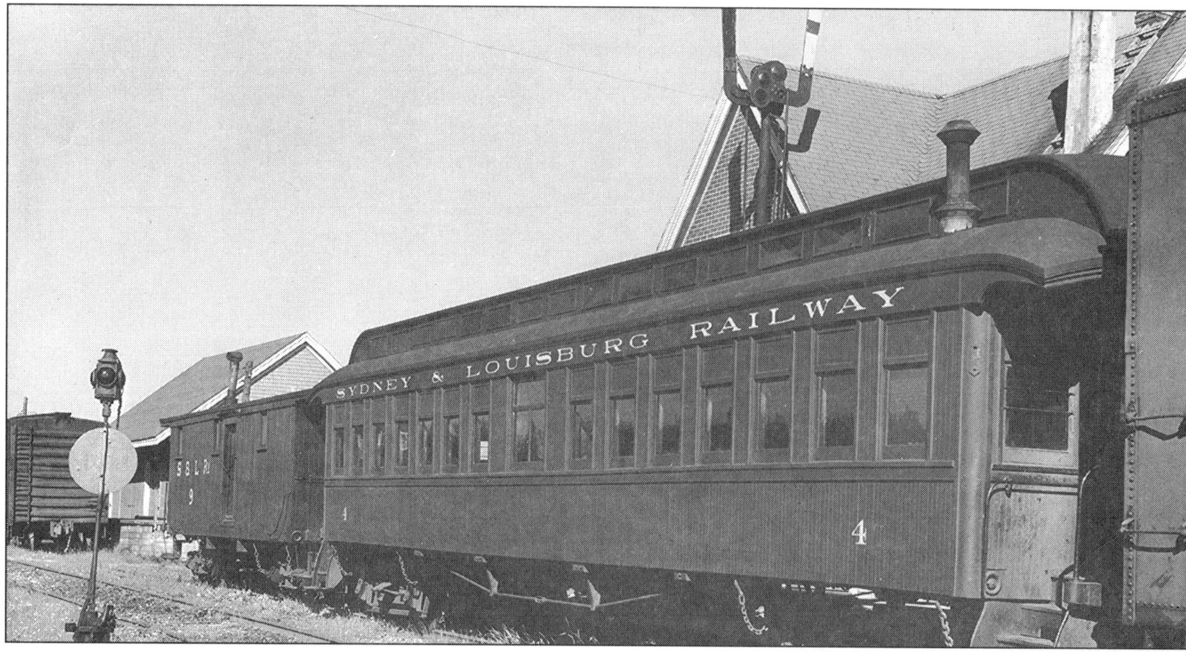

At Clark's Siding, heading to Louisbourg. [S&LRHSoc.]

Coach #4 at Louisbourg. This is an older model coach, wooden framed with truss rods. Dating around 1890 this coach is now at the Canadian Railway Museum, St. Constant, Que. [S&LRHSoc.]

Records and Telegraphs

Every train load of coal had to be weighed and recorded, and in the S&L's heyday that meant a mountain of paperwork. At times during the war years of the 1940s, trains were arriving at the International Piers every 15 minutes. By 1950, the S&L was still one of the Canadian Railway Association's top performers. In the month of October 1950, the S&L averaged 42.8 tons of freight per car mile, more than any other railroad in Canada for the period.

From the beginning, S&L operations were linked by means of Morse telegraphy. The Louisbourg station, for instance, contained a telegraph office.

The organized chatter of dots and dashes undecipherable to anyone but a trained dispatcher was used to communicate between the various stations and to keep the trains running on time. S&L stations eventually became the outlets for the public telegraph system which was commonly used for long distance communication even after telephones were available.

Many people can still recall the impact of receiving a telegram. Delivered to the customer's door by a company messenger, telegrams were written in a cryptic and distinctive style. Because of the cost, they were used sparingly by most people, usually when a letter was just too slow. Bearing urgent news of births, deaths, engagements and the like, they were often received with a mixture of anticipation and dread. Telegrams held a certain ceremonial value and often became a tangible record of momentous family events.

Freight and Passengers Too!

Although first and foremost a carrier of Cape Breton coal, the S&L, in compliance with its government charter, was also a freight and passenger line. Freight, at one time, generated upwards of 25 per cent of the railway's revenue. Longtime S&L employee John O'Neill, now a Devco Railway engineer, can recall the train delivering almost all the freight that arrived in his hometown of Glace Bay. Everything from food stuffs and furniture to automobiles and funeral caskets. Local truckers completed the transport and delivery.

Freight that was less than a full freight car (LCL) was off loaded at the Glace Bay freight shed, regrouped and then sent on to Louisbourg and other stops along the line. For outgoing

The Sydney and Louisburg road have added another handsome combination baggage and passenger car to their already heavy rolling stock. The car arrived at Sydney, Friday and was manufactured by Rhodes, Curry & Co., Amherst.

— Announcement in the SYDNEY DAILY POST, July 15, 1902. Rhodes & Curry Co. were premier builders of that era, having been prime contractor on Beinn Bhreagh, Alexander Graham Bell's estate at Baddeck.

❖ ❖ ❖

[There was] a change of management in the superintendent's office and the board of directors . . . said we weren't getting coal out fast enough. So they ordered 100 of the 100-ton cars . . . This railroad went out and ballasted it for 40-ton cars . . . They didn't know anything about it and they were too important to ask anybody anything. The first trip they made when the new cars came in, they sent 60 down to New Waterford and loaded them at the No. 12 colliery and when they got them loaded — diesels were in then, steam locomotives were gone — they sent three diesels down to take that train of coal to the international pier . . . halfway between New Waterford and Victoria Junction, the railroad fell apart . . . The cars were twisted and turned . . . When they got the whole thing straightened up, out of 60 cars they had onto the fella, they scrapped 39 of them. They were brand new. First run. That ended that.

— Recollection of GUY HILTZ

❖ ❖ ❖

freight, the process was reversed. Supply or "material" trains for the collieries were another aspect of the S&L freight service.

Other rolling stock on the S&L line included a variety of box cars, cabooses, flat cars, snow ploughs, flangers, gondolas and the ubiquitous hopper cars, the workhorse of the railway. Most were built by the Eastern Car Company of Trenton, Nova Scotia. The S&L conducted a continuous upgrade of their hopper car fleet, one of the last big orders was delivered by Eastern Car in 1951. The original hoppers were all wood construction with a small capacity of six tons. By 1911, steel units of 40-ton capacity were standard. Around 1927, 50-ton units were common. By the 1960s, 65-ton capacity hoppers were being used. There were even some capable of carrying 100 tons, sometimes with disastrous results.

Before paved, all-weather roads and the family car were common, the train was the mainstay for many travellers during the first part of the 20th century. Especially in the winter and spring, it was easier and more reliable to take the train. During the 1920s and 1930s, as Cletus Egan recalls, travel by car could be quite a challenge. A single track with deep, frozen ruts made two-way traffic difficult. To remedy the situation, many drivers resorted to carrying a pick-axe in the trunk of their cars. When they met an oncoming vehicle, out would come the pick-axe. One driver or the other would chop his way out of the frozen ruts to the safety of the siding, wait there momentarily until his challenger passed, bounce back into the ruts, and carry on his way. Protocol as to who did the chopping and who waited until the path was clear was decided on the spot.

Under such conditions, many found the trains to be more convenient than automobile travel. Certainly the S&L filled that role for the communities in southeastern Cape Breton. Notoriously slow, the trains were nonetheless comfortable by the standards of the day. Even now, people remember the old train coaches with affection. Rose O'Neill, for instance, recalls the experience of her first trip in an S&L coach when she was 7-years old. As nightfall came, "the conductor made his rounds through the cars to light the coach lamps. I can remember the men sitting back smoking their pipes, reading the paper and everything was so quiet. I said something to my aunt and she put her finger to her mouth as much as to say: 'Keep quiet!' Quite different than it is today. If you're on a train with children now, you can't hear yourself." At the time, about 1914, Rose found the trip "just something out of this world."

A casual glance at an S&L timetable from 1935 reveals how thoroughly the company's trains connected the mining areas. In the beginning, stops were located every five miles regardless if anyone lived there or not! At one time there were 27 official stops on the S&L circuit. Some, like Louisbourg, Mira, Morien, Glace Bay, Bridgeport, Dominion and New Waterford, were full-service outlets with station houses, freight sheds and agents. Others — like Catalone, Milton and Homeville — were referred to as "flag stations," and had only a small waiting room or wooden platform for passengers and freight. Homeville originally had its own station house but it was later moved lock, stock and barrel, up the line to Mira.

On occasion, passengers could even "hitch" a train ride if they were not at a regular station. Stopping in the "middle of nowhere" to drop off passengers for a day's trout fishing or berry picking was common. This casual approach to railroading led some wags to nickname the S&L the "Slow and Lazy" railway, but the relaxed pace was actually dictated by speed regulations. Trains rarely topped 20 miles an hour in compliance with the rules of the road.

If "Slow and Lazy" seems like an unkind nickname, don't be fooled. Some rail lines received far more critical designations. The Halifax and Southwestern Railway, for instance, was dubbed the "Hellish Slow and Wobbly". Worse still was Port Arthur, Duluth and Western Railway. This line picked up the moniker "Poverty, Agony, Distress and Want."

The Brownhoist Crane from the defunct Chicnecto Ship Railway Co. It was built in the 1880's and saw a great deal of service at S&L construction and derailment scenes. *[S&LRHSoc.]*

By comparison with the regular passenger service, the hobos or "man trains" as they were called, were considerably less comfortable. These were 50-foot long box cars with high windows and wooden bench seats stretched like church pews along either side. The company used them to shuttle miners to and from the collieries. One concession to comfort on the "man trains" was steam heat piped in from the locomotive's boiler during cold weather. Despite their utilitarian appearance, they were always given the right-of-way over most other trains on the S&L line. Getting the miners to work on time was a priority for the Dominion Coal Company. In 1913, ridership on the S&L reached a high of 176,000 passengers. Miners using the "man trains" accounted for a good portion of that figure.

SYDNEY AND LOUISBURG RAILWAY

TIME TABLE No. 52

TAKING EFFECT 12 01 A. M. Mon. Sept. 30th, 1935

For Use of Employees Only

Destroy Former Time Tables

WEST BOUND TRAINS 102	100	96	94	92	90	Telegraph Calls	Station Nos.	STATIONS	Distance from Sydney	Coal, Scale, Water Turntable	EAST BOUND TRAINS 91	93	95	97	101	103
EXPRESS Saturdays Only	EXPRESS Saturdays Only	EXPRESS Saturdays Only	Mixed Daily except Sunday	EXRESS Saturdays Only	Mixed Daily except Sunday						Mixed Daily except Sunday	EXPRESS Saturdays Only	Mixed Daily except Sunday	EXRESS Saturdays Only	EXPRESS Saturdays Only	EXPRESS Saturdays Only
A. M.	P. M.	P. M.	A. M.	P. M.	P. M.	P	0	INTERNATIONAL PIER	2.2	WSC	A. M.	P. M.	P. M.	P. M.	P. M.	P. M.
								2.2								
					2.30	S. F.	1	Arr. SYDNEY Dep. N	0.0	Y'S CT	8.30					
								1.5								
					2.18	B. R.	2	SYDNEY JUNCTION	1.5		8.42					
								1.5								
					2.13	A. S.	4	ASSEMBLY YARD	3.0		8.47					
								1.0								
					1.55	PY.	5	VICTORIA JUNCTION N	4.0	W	9.05					
								3.0								
					1.48	K.	8	OLD TANK	7.0		9.12					
								1.5								
					1.43		10	GARDINER	8.5		9.17					
								1.5								
					1.25	MO DY	11	DOMINION N	10.0	W	9.35					
								2.0								
					1.10	B.	13	BRIDGEPORT D	12.0		9.50					
								2.0								
					1.05	HU	14	HUB JUNCTION D	14.0	WS	9.55					
								1.0								
12.05	8.05	10.30	9.40	6.30	1.00	CH	15	GLACE BAY N	15.0	WCT	10.?0	5.15	2.45	9.20	6.45	10.45
								1.0								
12.00	8.00	10.25	9.37	6.25		CA	16	CALEDONIA JUNCTION	16.0	WS		5.20	2.50	9.25	6.50	10.50
								5.0								
11.45	7.45		9.22			RN	21	MORIEN JUNCTION D	21.0				3.12		7.05	11.05
								4.0								
			9.09				23	HOMEVILLE	25.0				3.30			
								0.5								
			9.07			ON	24	MILTON	25.5				3.32			
								3.0								
			8.50			RA	28	MIRA D	28.5	W			3.42			
								2.0								
			8.35				29	DIXON'	30.5				3.52			
								2.5								
			8.30				33	CATALONE	33.0				4.00			
								2.0								
			8.25			CR	35	CLARK'S	35.0				4.05			
								4.0								
			8.15			BU	40	Dep. LOUISBURG Arr. D.	39.0	W C S			4.15			
P. M.	P. M.	P. M.	A. M.	P. M.	P. M.						A. M.	P. M.	P. M.	P. M.	P. M.	P. M.

VICTORIA BRANCH

106	Telegraph Calls	Station Nos.	STATIONS	Distance from Sydney		105
MIXED Daily ex. Sund'y						MIXED Daily ex. Sund'y
A. M.						A. M.
9.00	FY	5	Arr. VICTORIA JUNCT. Dep. N	4.0		9.15
			6.0			
8.40	S	6	SUMMIT	10.0		9.35
			1.5			
8.25	WA	7	Dep. WATERFORD Arr. D	11.5	WCS	9.45
A. M.						A. M.

NUMBER SIX BRANCH

96	92	Telegraph Calls	Station Nos.	STATIONS	Distance from Sydney	93	97
EXPRESS Saturdays Only	EXPRESS Saturdays Only					EXPRESS Saturdays Only	EXPRESS Saturdays Only
P. M.	P. M.					P. M.	P. M.
10.25	6.25	CA.	16	Arr. CALEDONIA JUNCT. Dep.	16.0	5.20	9.25
				6.0			
10.00	6.00		17	Dep. NUMBER SIX Arr.	22.0	5.45	9.50
P. M.	P. M.					P. M.	P. M.

MORIEN BRANCH

102	100	Telegraph Calls	Station Nos.	STATIONS	Distance from Sydney	101	103
EXPRESS Saturdays Only	EXPRESS Saturdays Only					EXPRESS Saturdays Only	EXPRESS Saturdays Only
P. M.	P. M.					P. M.	P. M.
11.25	7.25	RN.	21	Arr. MORIEN JUNCTION Dep.	21.0	7.05	11
				2.0			
11.15	7.15		22	Dep. MORIEN Arr	23.0	7.15	11.15
P. M.	P. M.					P. M.	P. M.

"D"—Day Telegraph Office.

Sydney to Louisburg, Victoria Junction to Waterford, Caledonia Junction to Number Six and Morien Junction to Morien is East.

"N"—Day and Night Telegraph Office

Timetable, 1935. [S&LRHSoc.]

By the 1950s, passenger service on the S&L was on the wane. Some wooden coaches were unable to pass new regulations requiring steel-centre beams. They became prized acquisitions for collectors like Chadwell O'Connor of Alta Loma, California, who made an offer on one of the cars in 1960.

[The Hobo or Man Trains] were given a priority although they weren't running on any special train order. But you knew they were man trains and you stayed out of their way. The dispatcher as a rule kept you out of their way. They'd tell you — "Well, wait and let the man train go." If the men didn't get to the pit on time to get the first rake, they were growling. They'd have to wait a while for the rake to come back up. Once they got to the bottom of the mine they could get to the place of work. It was room and pillar a lot of it at that time. Same way coming up. They'd want to get the first rake to get up to the wash house to get the hottest water for a shower. Then when they got the shower, you had to have the engine on the man cars with steam on them and warmed up because when the men came out — the first rake when they came up — especially in the winter, if you didn't have your cars warmed up, they'd be growling. You know, they'd growl at the conductor first and then the conductor would growl at the trainmen! But you always managed to get your work done so you could have the steam on for about 20 minutes and you could heat those cars up pretty quick.

— longtime trainman John O'Neill recalling the "man trains" on the S&L line.

Coupling and Braking

The blight of every brakeman's life in the early days of railroading was the link and pin coupling system. The link and pin method was the cause of a great many injuries and death. The coupling was made as one rail car approached another, sometimes at considerable speed. The link — hanging loosely down at an angle of about 30 degrees — had to be lifted up and guided into a socket on the drawbar of the approaching car, at which point a pin dropped through the center to lock the two together. Conversely, to separate the cars the pin had to be removed. Both maneuvers required speed and dexterity. During winter freeze-ups or even brief moments of inattention, it could result in disaster. Many brakemen had fingers crushed or severed in the process. Coupling meant that the brakeman had to dodge in and out between train cars that were still rolling. Getting caught up in the machinery could mean death.

Brakes were another bugaboo. Early trains had hand brakes on each car that were controlled by a standpipe and wheel mounted at the top end of each rail car. A brakeman had to leap from cartop to cartop, stand precariously on a narrow footboard and wind brakes on and off as the train made its way up and down the various grades. Executing this maneuver was tricky at the best of times. Done at night during a Cape Breton winter, it could be treacherous.

In 1939 the handbrakes of four coal cars were released prematurely a half-mile from the town coal pier on a grade. The cars sailed off the end of the pier. [S&LRHSoc.]

In the U.S., air-brakes were given their first trials in 1868, but were not perfected and put into wide use until 1887. In that year, George Westinghouse Jr. invented the triple valve mechanism which revolutionized air-brake technology. He gave practical demonstrations of his new system across the country and air-brakes became standard equipment on most railways shortly thereafter. By 1885, there were over four thousand patents on file for automatic couplers, most of them impractical. But just a few years later railroad authorities in Canada and the United

In 1912, S&L engineer Parker Holmes of Glace Bay, driving No. 56, narrowly averted taking the life of a 2-year old who had wandered on the tracks. Mr. Parker had just rounded a curve beyond the Bridgeport Station when he spotted the toddler about 100 yards ahead, walking the tracks. There was no time to lose. After sounding the whistle and applying the brakes, the driver closed the throttle and ran out of the engine. He then slid down the pilot just in time to save the child.

❖ ❖ ❖

States approved a design and automatic couplers became a welcome addition to life on the railroad.

The S&L line was slow to adopt the changing technology, though by about 1915, automatic couplings came into common use. Air brakes were adopted a few years later. These were major innovations that improved the lot of everyone involved with railroading; much to the relief of S&L railwaymen.

It was quite common when the link and pin was the means of coupling the cars to have breakaways which sometimes caused pile-ups and derailments. The most difficult coupling or hitch to make was between an automatic and "bullhead" as the link and pin was called. Quite a number of the trainmen who worked with the link and pin had part of their fingers pinched off. I'm fortunate in having all my fingers with me today.

Our cars and locomotives were not equipped with air brakes. We had to brake the trains by hand on the grades. This was quite hazardous, especially with snow or freezing rain. There were three grades on which we had to brake between the mines where we would get our train and Louisburg.

— CHARLIE BAGNELL, who began working for the S&L at age 14. Mr. Bagnell worked on the line for half a century, mostly as a conductor, though he was yardmaster at the time of his retirement in 1967.

CHAPTER SEVEN

The End . . . and a Beginning

From its birth to its death, the fate of the S&L Railway was tied to that of the coal industry.

The line had been created quite simply out of a desire to transport coal to its winter port (Louisbourg). With the decline in the coal trade after World War II it was inevitable that the S&L would feel the effects. The freight and passenger service of the S&L, even in the best of times, never accounted for more than 25 per cent of the company's revenue. By 1960 — with better roads and many more cars and trucks — that figure declined to about 3 per cent. Clearly, the railway would not have a future if the coal industry was not thriving.

Looking Back

In the early years of the S&L Railway, a tremendous infusion of capital by the Dominion Coal Company and subsidies by the federal government meant that the railroad enjoyed "state of the art" technology in many of its facilities. Strong demand for coal in the New England and Montreal markets meant brisk business for the railroad and the ports it served. Sydney was burgeoning and Louisbourg operated year round.

The building of the Sydney steel plant in 1900 brought increased prosperity, a boom that was felt throughout the industrialized corner of the island. Nearby mining towns grew up, often at a rapid pace. For example, by 1913, just six years after DOMCO opened its first mine shaft at New Waterford, the town had a population of more that 5000. The S&L laid down a new spur line to carry away the new mines' production. Waves of immigration brought labourers, merchants and craftsmen with European and Middle Eastern backgrounds. They set up their shops in towns like Louisbourg, Glace Bay and Sydney.

In 1910 the Dominion Coal Company split off its rail division and incorporated it as a wholly owned subsidiary, becoming the "Sydney and Louisburg Railway Company." The name change was a mere formality for most people, as the "S&L" had been in common usage for many years. Technically, S&L workers were employees of a separate company. In practical terms, of course, they were affected by everything that went on in the coal industry.

During the 1930s everyone felt the bite of the worldwide economic depression. Anyone who lived through that era has more than a few survival stories. Throughout the period the S&L chugged along at a much reduced rate. Every employee hustled to pick up whatever work was available. The chance to fill in on Christmas Day or take a night shift at a moment's notice was a welcome, but all too infrequent event. Still, people remember acts of kindness as men waived their seniority rights and passed work along to someone in need of a "shift" to feed their families or purchase a gift.

As the fighting intensified in World War II, Cape Breton became a major assembly point for ships of the wartime convoys. Availability of coal and steel was a major reason. In a scramble to meet the almost insatiable demand for fuel, coal trains began arriving at local shipping piers, sometimes at the rate of one every 15 minutes. More than 6,000 ships sailed from Sydney harbour between 1940 and 1945. Louisbourg regained its old edge as an ice-free port; its shipping piers were busy 12 months of the year, something not seen with regularity since the 1920s.

Ship repair was another aspect of the wartime demands. Sydney Engineering and Drydock became a beehive of activity, and L.H. Cann's Louisburg Ship Repair Plant employed 150 workers refitting warships and freighters including those of the Dominion Coal Company fleet. Both harbours were outfitted with anti-submarine nets. Such precautions were not taken without good cause. German U-boats cruised the coastline. The Newfoundland ferry *Caribou* was sunk in the Gulf of St. Lawrence in 1942, and four of the ships on charter to the Dominion Coal company were torpedoed while taking on cargo in Newfoundland ports.

The post-war years brought a renewed degree of prosperity to Cape Breton. Troops returned from Europe; home construction gained momentum; and the baby boom generation began making its appearance.

In the early 1950s, there was still a strong demand for coal. That meant workers held their own in terms of employment at the mines and on the railroad. At the S&L, management felt secure enough about the future to order 100 new hopper cars from the Eastern Car Works in

Trenton. The cars were delivered in 1951. That brought the S&L fleet of coal cars to 1050 with several hundred more on lease from other companies.

A profile of the S&L operation in 1959 shows it covered 116.03 miles of tracks, with freight totals in the range of 4,000,000 tons. The movement of coal accounted for 97 per cent of that total. There were 400 people on the payroll and there were 31 locomotives on the S&L roster, all coal-fired and steam-driven. One engine built in 1891 was still in service at the venerable age of 68.

Even in today's marketplace, people dream of attracting an industry of that size and profitability. But the Sydney and Louisburg Railway operated in the shadow of its high-profile cousins, the steel and coal industries. As a result, it often went about its daily routine almost unnoticed. Longtime railroaders recall jokingly that the only time Cape Bretoners noticed the S&L was when the train held them up at the Prince Street crossing in Sydney or on Main Street in Glace Bay.

Depending on where one was on the S&L's seniority list and call board, the 1950s might not have been a bad time on the railroad. Pay scales for S&L trainmen were comparable with those of the CN Railway and many senior workers "never missed a shift." Working for a "short line" railway had the added advantage of never having to contend with long road trips. CNR crews were often away from home for days. Barring major winter storms or some other calamity, S&L staffers were back in their beds every night.

A Hint of Things to Come

In the larger scheme of things, an underlying statistic was beginning to have an impact. At the beginning of the 1950s, coal supplied 52 per cent of Canada's energy demands. By 1957, the importation of cheap oil from the Middle East had reduced that figure to just 25 per cent. That same year, there was another ominous event closer to home. The Dominion Steel and Coal Company, DOSCO, was taken over by Hawker Siddley, a giant British-based group of companies. For Cape Breton, it proved to be an uneasy association.

Slowly, even the S&L showed signs of the coming trend. Having resisted acquiring diesel engines for many years, the railway finally gave in. The first four diesel locomotives were brought on line in 1960. Soon, six more were added; by the end of the following year, the

About face! Steam engine #42 and #12 are towed away by a diesel locomotive in 1955. This was an ominous sign of things to come. [S&LRHSoc.]

transition was complete. Engines No. 88 and No. 90 chugged into Glace Bay's Union Street Station on Friday afternoon, November 17, 1961. Their final trip marked a major milestone. The era of steam locomotion on the S&L had come to a close.

Two months earlier, in September 1961, the S&L had undergone another transition. The Canadian Senate enacted Bill — S19, merging the S&L with the Cumberland Railway Company, a deactivated division of the Dominion Steel and Coal Company. It is one of the few cases of a defunct company taking over an active, profitable railroad. The explanation most commonly offered goes this way: The terms of the Maritime Freight Rates Act of 1927 granted subsidized rates to railways operating on a federal charter in the region east of Levis, Quebec. The Cumberland Railway held such a charter. On the other hand, the S&L operated under provincial mandate. For many years, an Act of the Governor-in-Council had extended the equalization payments to the S&L but that was open to debate with a change of government

These passenger cars, veterans of a better day, lie alongside the main line in Morien. [S&LRHSoc.]

or intervention by another party. Bringing the S&L under the umbrella of the Cumberland company charter made it automatically eligible for the federal benefits and placed it in a more secure position. It became officially the Sydney and Louisburg Railway division of the Cumberland Railway Company. Unimpressed with the legal niceties, people throughout the region and those who worked on the line, stuck with the old, familiar "The S&L."

The coal industry entered a definite slump. By 1962, coal exports at Louisbourg had declined to a point where the shipping pier was considered uneconomical to operate. It was dismantled and scrapped. A contributing factor in Louisbourg's decline as a winter port was the advent of the ice-breaking service by the Canadian Coast Guard. Massive new ships with enough power to ram their way through all but the thickest ice, were put in service to facilitate traffic to the newly developed St. Lawrence Seaway system, and to keep ports in Newfoundland and Nova Scotia open all winter long.

On the home front, further signs of the changing times occurred when the DOSCO coal yard, which for decades had supplied domestic fuel to Louisbourg, was closed. Thereafter, all coal orders had to be trucked to the town. With the increased use of private automobiles and the construction of all weather roads, ridership on the S&L shrank to almost nothing. Finally, in March 1963, all passenger service on the line was discontinued.

The decline in the coal industry accelerated in the mid-1960s. In 1967 the giant Hawker Siddley Corporation announced its withdrawal from the Cape Breton coal fields, and its intended closure of the Sydney steel plant, a day many Cape Bretoners now recall as "Black Friday."

The last run to Louisbourg. In April 1968 the final load of coal was delivered to the National Sea Products fishplant. They had converted to oil heating. L. Bill Jones, engineer; R. John Skinner conductor.[S&LRHSoc.]

Winding Down

A few months prior to "Black Friday" (October 13, 1967), a much more low-key event was taking place. The Cumberland Railway Company made an application to the Board of Transport Commissioners of Canada for abandonment of its railway line between Broughton Junction and Louisbourg. The distance was approximately 12 miles. Hearings were held at Louisbourg, with many interventions presented, including one from Gordon Cameron, a retired veteran employee of the S&L. Mr Cameron spoke on behalf of the town's Board of Trade.

The intervenors argued with conviction and passion. The company countered with cold, hard statistics. Some showed the cost estimates of needed repairs to the Broughton-Louisbourg line. The company speculated it would have to spend $707,000 in order to guarantee its future operation. Much of the money was targeted for the sea wall at Mira, the Mira River bridge, and smaller bridge installations along the route.

In an attempt to halt the slide in the island's economy, the Government of Canada commissioned an economist, Dr. J.R. Donald to write a report on the "Cape Breton Coal Problem." The *Donald Report* resulted in legislation: Bill C-135, An Act to Incorporate the

Cape Breton Development Corporation. The bill emphasized a down-sizing of the coal industry, retraining the miners, and a turn to smaller community-based industries. Comprehensive in its detail, the report contained absoutely no provision for the maintenance of the rail line to Louisbourg. The legislation passed through Parliament in March 1968, and the Cape Breton Development Corporation, DEVCO, became a reality.

The Sydney and Louisburg Railway was folded into the coal division of DEVCO and renamed the DEVCO Railway. Such an entity survives and prospers today within that corporation.

And so it came to pass that the old familiar S&L name was officially erased from the rolling stock and the letterhead. The passenger service had already been eliminated, and the rails to Louisbourg lifted and sold for scrap. Hence, the S&L of yesteryear exists only in memory. But there are those who can still recall a time in Cape Breton when a wave of your hand could bring an entire train to a halt. And in those early days, for train crews and passengers alike, a ride on the S&L was not just a means of transportation. More often than not, it was a ticket to adventure.

A New Life . . . as a Museum

Keeping alive the memories of the S&L Railway passed to a group of dedicated people: the members of the Sydney and Louisburg Railway Historical Society.

In 1968, the Dominion Coal Company deeded the S&L Station and the surrounding property to the Town of Louisbourg. The building was occupied briefly as a medical clinic by the late Dr. J.G.B. Lynch, but then the structure fell into disrepair. By 1971, boarded up windows and peeling paint blighted the architecture of its simple and lovely "carpenter Gothic" exterior. On the inside, rising damp had taken its toll on the plaster walls and ceilings. In a word, it was a mess.

A grassroots group of S&L retirees took note of what was happening to the old building and did what they could to halt the downward slide in the station's condition. Guy Hiltz and his brother Jim, Gordon Cameron, Charlie Bagnell and anyone else the group could "put the arm on," like Charlie's son-in-law, Neil MacLean, took up mops and paintbrushes and set to work. Guy Hiltz recalls how they talked among themselves about the possibility of rescuing some of the old equipment from the roundhouse at Glace Bay. The age of steam had passed and all steam-related equipment was headed "the way of all flesh."

Guy Hiltz and Gordon Cameron approached the S&L/DEVCO Superintendent with their request. In Guy's words, we thought "We'll go in and ask him, he can't kill us." When told of the mission they were on the Superintendent was tickled to death that we were going to do that and he said to see Joe Fisher and tell Joe Fisher to give you whatever you want. Joe took a great interest in it. He was a very helpful man. He's the fella that gave us the light out of the passenger car. He said 'why not take the light out of the passenger car and put it in here so people can see it.' Gordon Cameron wired it up. It was supposed to take oil, but no one would dare put oil on those shades. He gave us two stoves as well. Different shacks along the road would have one of them but when they tore down the shacks, they saved some of the stoves. They were brand new, pretty well, and so he asked us one day and then sent them right out here, you didn't fool around with him . . . he sent them out on the company truck; two fellas with them. They'd stay with you and unload and everything, put it where you wanted it. Joe Fisher was good to you in that way. They took an interest in it. That's what I say about railroad men. They're a clannish tribe. But if you got a good railroad man, you've got a good man. So that's how we got an awful lot of this stuff.

Ann Terry MacLellan, Director of Tourism at DEVCO, answered their request for painting supplies. So as Guy Hiltz puts it "We painted every — thing in sight." Soon, others, like John Fortier, then the Superintendent of the Fortress of Louisbourg National Historic Site, became involved. Eventually, applications for financial assistance were made to a variety of community development agencies. Grant money was secured and the restoration project entered another phase.

The weekly *Cape Breton Highlander*, in August 1971, reported that "Since its retirement as the eastern terminus of the S&L Railroad, the old station at Louisbourg has been the eye of the hurricane in tempestuous battles for possession, involving at various times Town Council, the Cape Breton Regional Planning Commission and a candlestick maker named Jones from British Columbia." The item went on to report that Louisbourg's Beautification Committee had given the final word on the fate of the 75-year old structure. Work was under way to restore and reopen the local landmark as a multi-use town center.

Several months later, the *Highlander* carried a follow-up story complete with a photo of the newly restored station and a caption that read **"You mean that's the old Louisburg**

station?" The building, the newspaper noted, "had almost completed its Cinderella act" and next spring it would step out as a completely refurbished town center. The fairy godmother to the project was the Louisbourg Beautification Committee, composed of townspeople, S&L retirees and railway buffs and restoration experts from the Fortress of Louisbourg. The same group would later incorporate themselves (in 1973) as the S&L Railway Historical Society.

The first meeting of the Sydney and Louisburg Railway Historical Society was held on December 17, 1971. The first executive included William Lewis, President; John Fortier, Secretary; Gordon Cameron, Vice-President; and Jim How, Curator. Within the next few years the society began to expand and so did the collections (artifacts, pictures and memorabilia).

Getting the old S&L station back into shape included replacing the roof, re-plastering walls, rebuilding two chimneys (a third, not part of the original station, was torn down), glazing the windows and making the plumbing operational again. Every effort was made to keep all the work authentic to the late Victorian period of the station's history.

The newly plastered walls were barely dry and there was still much to be done to the grounds when the restored S&L station was ready for its re-dedication on the 77th Anniversary of its opening, June 17, 1972. The evening ceremony included an address by Bob Chisholm, director of the Cape Breton Tourist Association. Mayor George Lewis drove a ceremonial "last spike" to mark the occasion. Turn-of-the-century songs and music were provided by The Eastern Gentlemen barbershop quartet and the 30-piece Sydney Mines Legion Band.

Jim How, a former director of the Glace Bay Miners Museum and then Head of Interpretation at the Fortress of Louisbourg as well as volunteer curator of the S&L museum thanked everyone involved in the project for their generosity. He noted that "numerous individuals have given photographs and furnishings. We couldn't have established this building as a museum without their help."

A MISSED OPPORTUNITY

When diesel engines came on line at the S&L, the old steam locomotives were made obsolete, though several were in excellent condition. As the Company could find no profitable market for them, they established a locomotive graveyard at New Waterford. The great iron beasts, the pride of former days met an ignominious end; they were cut up for scrap.

Guy Hiltz tells of a missed opportunity to secure one of the machines for the S&L Railway Museum in Louisbourg. It is enough to make fans of the age of steam cry real tears.

"We could have had a locomotive here when they scrapped all these steel locomotives back in the nineteen sixties. Alex MacDonald was superintendent then — he took over from D.W. MacDonald, and I was mayor of the town then. So he came up one day and he told me they're going to scrap these locomotives. Why don't you get one for Louisbourg?" "Will you give us one", I asked him? MacDonald said, "Sure, I'll give you any one you want."

And so I told them that in council. "Well blessed God! There was a deathly calm that came over that council for about five minutes, and then the three holes in the roof you see there, that's where three of them went through. They wouldn't hear tell of it. Cost you a fortune to keep it painted and the kids would tear it apart . . . Oh Lord God Almighty, it was terrible!"

"We could have had that locomotive and she was just out of the shop after a complete overhaul, and the overhaul cost one hundred and twenty thousand dollars at that time, and he said it was in perfect shape. They wouldn't hear tell of it. But to think that locomotive came out like that; out of that shop and she made one run to Sydney with a train of coal, and came back to Glace Bay, and there was an engine there waiting for her, took a hold of her and towed her over to Caledonia Yard and scrapped her."

"Now, they're hooting and hollering today 'We should've had a steam locomotive.' Sure you should've had a steam locomotive. Go and talk to them fellas. But think of what an attraction that would be today if you had a steam locomotive."

The S&L Museum Today

The spirit of teamwork and generosity that gave birth to the formation of the S&L Railway Historical Society still prevails. The collection has grown ten-fold over the years and exhibits are still being donated. People continue to display a keen interest in keeping memories of the S&L "on track."

Between June 26 and the end of July 1972, over 6000 people visited the new museum and tourist center. In an interview with the *Cape Breton Post*, William Lewis, then president of the local society, assessed the first year's operation and deemed it a great success. The placement of the tourist information centre in the museum had been a "mutually beneficial relationship," Lewis said. "We hope to make this a place for loafers," he added. "We want it to become a focal point for the community the way it always was — someplace where we can greet visitors to Louisbourg and the railroad men can come to swap stories."

Almost a quarter of a century later, the S&L Museum and the society that gave it renewed life are still going strong. The freight shed, once in the hands of a private owner, has been returned and restored to its original condition. It now holds pride of place next to the station house. A short length of rails was laid and a caboose, box car and some rolling stock have been added. There is even hope of resurrecting one of the original locomotives. Artifacts and photographs have been catalogued and exhibits are being continually enhanced. A constitution and by-laws have long since been adopted, and the Museum has been accredited as a "Local Exhibit Centre" by the Board of Governors of the Nova Scotia Museum in 1976. In May 1989, the station-house was designated a Provincial Heritage Property of Nova Scotia.

Many of the above advances, so briefly mentioned, required an enormous amount of work by the volunteers. Much of the work was unglamorous, but all of it has been necessary to the longterm success of the group.

Membership in the S&L Railway Historical Society numbers in the hundreds, and there is a program of events. One of the program highlights is the reunion held at the station every September. It makes a perfect backdrop for a day of reminiscing about life on the S&L. Activities are not restricted to the summer tourist season, for monthly meetings are held year round. The society keeps its membership up-to-date with an informative newsletter.

The present officers of the society include Honorary President Guy Hiltz, President

Guy M. Hiltz stands at the rails of the station which he has seen in its prime. [S&LRHSoc.]

William Bussey, Vice-President Donald Skinner, Secretary Jean Kyte, Treasurer Margie Cameron, and Curator Eugene Magee. On the Board of Directors are Charlie Stacey, Wilson Levy, Jim MacKay, Charles Blanchard, Harvey MacLeod and Mayor Victor Hanham.

The passing years have shown the wisdom of those who fought to save the Sydney & Louisburg station from the fate that befell so much railway architecture across Canada. It now stands as the lone "survivor" of the S&L line. Moreover, a full century after the first steam locomotive huffed and puffed its way into Louisbourg, the station stands as a lasting memorial to those who kept the trains running. Thanks to the tireless work of the Railway Historical Society it appears certain, that this time round, the S&L will never run out of steam.

APPENDIX A

Locomotives

The unquestioned "stars" of the S&L Railway, and indeed of any steam railway, were its locomotives. The S&L line, because it was owned and developed by a mining company, had a ready supply of cheap coal. Consequently, it made good economic sense for the S&L to retain its coal-fired steam engines long after most other North American railroads had converted to diesel electric power. As a result, the S&L had an amazing array of locomotives over its long history; from tiny "yard goats" used for shunting to some of the largest steam engines in Canada.

On the original Gisborne/S&L road, motive power was provided by three Fairlie "double-enders." Like a child's push me — pull me toy, the Fairlies looked the same coming and going. They consisted of two 4-4-0 engines joined back to back under one long common boiler with a smoke stack on each end; a single firebox and a cab in the centre. They were designed and patented in 1864 by Robert Fairlie, superintendent of the Londonderry and Coleraine Railway in Ireland and manufactured by the Fox-Walker company of Bristol. Fairlie was a strong advocate of the narrow gauge (3 feet 4 inches) rail system. Few of these picturesque machines, however, were operated in North America. From the International Coal & Railway Company, the S&L inherited three steam engines, including a pair of handsome Rhode Island Forneys and the "A.C. Morton."

A popular practice in the early days of rail was the naming of coaches and locomotives after prominent people and places. This was likely a carry over from the shipping trade where vessels are christened and given a name at their launching. One of the first engines on the S&L roster was proudly emblazoned with the name A.C. Morton. Morton was an engineer who had worked for the General Strong Group at Bridgeport and between 1863-65 reorganized the company as the International Coal and Railway.

#23 alongside the freight shed in Louisbourg. "It was the only ___ engine they tried to keep clean." G.B. Hiltz. [S&LRHSoc.]

The "A.C. Morton," that operation's first locomotive, was an 0-6-0 tank engine built by the Hunslet Engine Company of England in 1870. It weighed nearly 20 tons, had 36-inch drivers and 12 by 20-inch cylinders. It worked the company's standard gauge railway between Old Bridgeport and the International Pier in Sydney.

Other S&L locomotives were named the Henry Day, Louisburg, Pepperrell, and the David MacKeen. One even bore the whimsical title "Pinkie." A small engine that projected a lot of personality, the Pinkie was the subject of a poem by Mrs. Ida MacAulay of Glace Bay. As a girl she had watched it work the rail line not far from her home. The poem was later set to music by Professor John O'Donnell, director of the Men of the Deeps choir and it became part of their repertoire.

Over time, locomotives lost their distinctive titles and were identified only by number. The "Pinkie," for example, became S&L engine #1 in 1901. In the same year, the "A.C. Morton" became S&L engine #3 and was retired in 1942.

The A.C. Morton, named after an early engineer and organizer of the International Coal and Railway Co.

[S&LRHSoc.]

D.W. MacDonald, S&L Superintendent from 1919 to 1952 began his career with the company in 1893 as a fireman. His longevity on the job led to a reputation among younger employees that he must have "come with the rails." Interviewed by the *Cape Breton Post* at the time of his retirement, MacDonald vividly recalled his first job with the S&L, which was, unloading rails arriving in Sydney Harbor from Scotland for the extension of the railway to Louisbourg. So he did quite literally "come with the rails." MacDonald, known throughout the company as "D.W.," became an engineer in 1896. His first locomotive was the "A.C. Morton."

In a custom that harkens back more than a century, the new Texas company, RailTex, that recently took over the Sydney to Truro section of the Canadian National Railways, has once again begun naming its locomotives. They have chosen a Scottish theme in keeping with the area's history and have used the names of famous Scottish writers like Robert Burns and Sir Walter Scott. The company logo is a lion rampant, another traditional Scottish emblem.

Most of the early locomotives on Cape Breton were imported from England. Later, others were purchased from manufacturers in Canada and the U.S. During the 1940s and 1950s, when many American railways were converting to diesel electric engines, the S&L picked up a number of their retired steam locomotives at fire sale prices.

D.W. MacDonald was the company's purchasing agent and made many trips to the U.S. and central Canada to inspect the S&L's new acquisitions. His sons, Bill and Rod MacDonald can still recall some of their father's stories about these forays, sometimes into Mississippi and the deep South. The train maintenance crew or "hostlers" as they were called in the trade would prepare the machines for their trip to Cape Breton. Often they filled the firebox and other storage compartments with spare parts as a bonus to "sweeten the deal." From MacDonald's standpoint, it was a very good deal. He recalled how the S&L had purchased entire locomotives for less than the original cost of the spare parts that had been thrown in free of charge. It made good economic sense for a company that could bunker those engines with coal from its own mines, which is precisely what the S&L did until the early 1960s. By doing so, the company's fuel costs, a make or break item on any transportation company's balance sheet, was kept remarkably low for most of the S&L's operating history.

#31 and #106 at Sydney Pier shops in 1959 show the difference in size of steam engines used on the S&L line.[S&LRHSoc.]

Railroad writer Bob Durning compiled a roster of S&L steam locomotives. His listing gives a clear profile of these key elements in the company's rolling stock.

The Locomotives

The S&L roster of steam locomotives is listed in two parts. The first classification is for the period from 1893 to 1901. There were 20 locomotives during that era, ranging from 0-4-0T to 2-8-4T. All were tank locomotives, with some being of the Forney type. The second classification is for 1901-1961, and it lists 71 locomotives with numbers from 1 to 106. Many of the 1893-1901 classification were renumbered in 1901 and five

#31, originally the H.M. Whitney. The noseplate and bell are on display in the S&L Railway Museum, Louisbourg, Nova Scotia. [S&LRHSoc.]

The famous Fairline double-ender

[S&LRHSoc.]

2-6-4T's were rebuilt to 2-6-0's with swinging tenders. No. 32 was rebuilt from a 2-6-4T to a 2-6-0 and then to a 0-6-0. Fourteen 2-8-2's, one 0-6-0 and twelve 0-8-0's were obtained second-hand from U.S. railways.

Several of the S&L "Mikado's" were larger than some of the C.N.R. engines operating in the area. No. 102, a 2-8-2, was the heaviest, weighing 311 tons, with a drawbar pull of approximately 54,700 pounds and a tractive effort of 60,000 pounds. This locomotive had the largest tender of any steam locomotive used in Canada. Many of the large tenders had to be reduced in size so drivers could see better when the locomotives were running backwards. This was particularly important at Louisbourg where there were no turning facilities and the engine had to make the return to Sydney in reverse. From a technical standpoint, this was not a problem. Steam locomotives operate with equal efficiency in either direction.

A rare photograph showing S&L employees, including a woman, Mary MacIntyre, telegrapher, on the #31. The S&L hired a number of women as telegraphers. [S&LRHSoc.]

Some of the U.S. railroads from which the S&L purchased locomotives from were: New York Central, Pierre Marquette; New Orleans, Mobile and Chicago; Pittsburgh and Lake Erie; Detroit and Toledo; Shoreline; Cambria; Indiana and Gulf and Mobile and Northern.

APPENDIX A

S&L Locomotive Classification

1893-1901

#1 PINKEY 0-4-0T built by Neilson (1868); re. S&L #1 (1901); scrapped 1930.

#2 HENRY DAY, 0-4-0T; Block & Hawthorne 1870; re. S&L #4 (1901); scrapped 1906.

#3 A.C. MORTON, 0-6-0T; Hunsel 1870; re. S&L #3 (1901); scrapped 1942.

#4 H.M. WHITNEY 2-6-4T; Rhode Island 1893; re. S&L #31 (1901); rebuilt to a 2-6-0 in 1949.

#5 SIR DONALD, 2-6-4T; Rhode Island 1893; re. S&L #32 (1901); rebuilt to a 2-6-0 1949.

#6 LOUISBURG, 2-4-4T; Rhode Island 1891; re. S&L #21 (1901); scrapped 1902.

#7 0-4-0T; Kingston 1863.

#8 E.F.ARCHIBALD. 0-6-0T; Baldwin 1889; re. S&L #2 (1901); scrapped 1925.

#9 2-4-4T; Schenectady 1900; re. S&L #23 (1901)

#10 Vacant.

#11 2-6-4T; Schenectady 1900' re. S&L #61 (1901); scrapped 1928.

#12 DAVID MacKEEN, 2-6-4T; Rhode Island 1894; re. S&L #33 (1901); scrapped 1951.

#13 SYDNEY, 2-6-4T; Rhode Island 1894; re. S&L #22 (1901); scrapped 1925.

#14 PEPPERAL, 2-6-4T; Rhode Island 1894; re. S&L #41 (1901); scrapped 1930.

#15 H.F. DIMOCK, 2-8-4T; Rhode Island 1896; re. S&L #50 (1901). scrapped 1930.

#16 2-8-4T; Schenectady 1899; re. S&L #62 (1901); scrapped 1930.

#17 2-6-4T; Schenectady 1899; re. S&L #42 (1901); rebuilt to 2-6-0 1949; sold to Acadia Coal Co. 1955, sold to Tibbets 1961; became part of S&L Steam railway 1970s.

#18 2-6-4T; Schenectady 1899; re. S&L #43 (1901); rebuilt to a 2-6-0 1949; leased to Cumberland Railway & Coal Co. 1955.

#19 2-6-4T; Schenectady 1900; re. S&L #44 (1901); scrapped 1936.
#20 0-4-0T; Schenectady 1901; re. S&L #5 (1901); scrapped 1924.
#21 2-8-4T; Schenectady 1901; re. S&L #63 (1901); scrapped 1929.

1901-1961

#1 PINKIE: 0-4-0T; Neilson #1366, 1867, ordered by Caledonia Coal & Railway Co. #1, scrapped 1930.
#2 HENRY DAY; 0-4-0T; Baldwin #9271, 1870, ordered by Glace Bay Mining #2, scrapped, 1924.
#3 A.C. MORTON; 0-6-0T; Hunslet #44, 1870, ordered by International Coal & Railway Co. #3, scrapped 1942.
#4 0-4-0T; Davenport #?, 1907, sold to Point Edward Quarries, 1927.
#5 0-4-0T; Schenectady #5790, 1901, ordered by Dominion Coal Co. #19, scrapped 1924.
#6 0-4-0T; Schenectady #5789, 1901, ordered by Dominion Coal Co. #6, scrapped 1924.
#7 0-6-2T; Taunton #526, 1871, ordered by Nova Scotia Coal Co. #4, bought by S&L 1924, scrapped 1933.
#8 0-4-0T; MLW #64708, 1923, ordered by Aluminium Co. of Canada #102, bought by S&L 1932, scrapped 1956.
#10 0-4-0T; MLW #40736, 1906, ordered by Eastern Car Co. #2.
#11 0-6-0; MLW #29874, 1904, ordered by Dominion Steel Co. #117
#12 0-6-0; MLW #29875, 1904, Dominion Steel Co. #118, renumbered Acadia Coal Co. #12
#13 0-6-0; MLW #42749, 1907, Dominion Steel Co. #112.
#14 0-6-0; MLW #45666, 1909, Dominion Steel Co. #119
#15 2-6-0; MLW #50140, 1911, Dominion Steel Co. re. 120 (1938) re. Acadian Coal Co. #14
#16 2-6-0; MLW #52783, 1913, ordered by Cumberland Railway & Coal Co. 1926, to S&L 1951, scrapped, 1952.
#17 2-6-4T; Alco (Schenectady) #27301, 1903, ordered by Nova Scotia Steel & Coal Co. #10
#18 0-6-0; Alco (Schenectady) #27302, 1903, ordered by Nova Scotia Steel & Coal Co. #11
#21 LOUISBOURG; 2-4-4T; Rhode Island #2623, 1891, ex S&L #5, scrapped 1902.
#22 SYDNEY; 2-4-4T; Rhode Island #3020, 1894, ex. S&L #12, scrapped 1925.
#23 2-4-4T; Alco (Schenectady) #5465, 1900, ex. S&L #8.

#31 2-6-4T; Rhode Island #2944, 1893, ex. S&L #3, rebuilt to 2-6- 0, 1950.

#32 2-6-4T; Rhode Island #2573, 1891, ex. S&L #4, rebuilt to 2-6-0 1950, later rebuilt to 0-6-0.

#33 2-6-4T; Rhode Island #3021, 1894, ex. S&L #11, rebuilt to 0-6-4T 1950.

#34 0-6-0; Davenport #?, 1925, ex. Dominion Steel & Coal Co. #116, bought by S&L 1949.

#41 PEPPERELL; 2-6-4T; Rhode Island #3063, 1895, ex. S&L #13, scrapped 1930.

#42 2-6-4T; Schenectady #5103, 1899, ex. S&L #16, rebuilt to 2-6-0, sold to Acadia Coal Co. 1946.

#43 2-6-4T; Schenectady #5104, 1899, ex. S&L #17, rebuilt to 2-6-0 1949, leased to Cumberland Railway & Coal co. 1955, scrapped 1958.

#44 2-6-4T; ALCO (Schenectady) #?, 1900, ex. S&L #18.

#45 2-6-4T; MLW #?, 1925, rebuilt to 2-6-0 1948.

#50 2-8-4T; Rhode Island #3127, 1896, ex. S&L #14, scrapped 1946.

#52 2-8-0; Alco (Brooks) #65978, 1924, Jefferson & Southwestern #52, bought by S&L 1924, leased to Cumberland Railway Co. 1944, scrapped 1959.

#55 2-8-0T; ALCO (Cooke) #28636, 1903, scrapped 1958.

#56 2-8-0T; ALCO (Cooke) #28637, 1903, scrapped 1959.

#57 2-8-0T; MLW #50148, 1911, scrapped 1959.

#58 2-8-0T; MLW #50946, 1912, scrapped 1954.

#59 2-8-0T; MLW #54393, 1914, scrapped 1928.

#61 2-8-4T ALCO (Schenectady) #5569, 1900, ex. S&L #10, scrapped 1928.

#62 2-8-4T; Alco (Schenectady) #5105, 1899, ex. S&L #15, scrapped 1930.

#63 2-8-4T; ALCO (Schenectady) #5791, 1900, ex S&L #20.

#70 2-8-2; MLW #66319, 1925.

#71 2-8-2; MLW #67622, 1928, Cambria & Indiania Railway #7, Bought by S&L 1941, scrapped 1957.

#72 2-8-2; Lima 5438, 1917, ex. New Orleans, Mobile & Chicago #104, ex. Tennessee, Alabama & Georgia #202, Gulf, Mobile & Northern, bought by S&L 1937.

#73 2-8-2; Baldwin #38354, 1912, ex. New Orleans, Mobile & Chicago, ex. Gulf, Mobile & Northern, ex. Tennessee, Alabama & Georgia #205, bought by S&L 1937.

#74 2-8-2; Baldwin #38355, 1912, ex. New Orleans, Mobile & Chicago #101, ex. Gulf, Mobile & Northern, ex. Tennessee, Alabama & Georgia #202, bought by S&L 1932.

#75 2-8-2 Baldwin #38373, 1912, ex. New Orleans, Mobile & Chicago #102, ex. Gulf, Mobile & Northern, ex. Tennessee, Alabama & Chicago #203, bought by S&L 1938, scrapped 1957.

#76 2-8-2; Baldwin 38378, 1912, ex. New Orleans, Mobile & Chicago #103, ex. Gulf, Mobile & Northern, ex. Tennessee, Alabama & Chicago #204, bought by S&L 1938.

#77 2-8-2; Baldwin #49239, 1918, ex. Cambria & Indiania #10, bought by S&L 1941, received new boiler 1950.

#78 2-8-2; Baldwin #49307, 1918, ex. Cambria & Indiania #11, bought by S&L 1941, scrapped 1957

#80 0-6-0; MLW #67237, 1927.

#81 0-6-0; MLW #67238, 1927.

#82 0-6-0; MLW #67623, 1928.

#83 0-6-0; Lima #1190, 1911, ex. Akron, Canton & Youngstown #1, bought by S&L 1930, scrapped 1958.

#84 0-8-0: ALCO (Pittsburgh) #59124, 1918, ex. Detroit & Toledo Shore Line #106, bought by S&L 1958.

#85 0-8-0; ALCO (Schenectady) #66397, 1925, ex. Detroit & Toledo Shore Line #110, bought by S&L 1954.

#86 0-8-0; ALCO (Brooks) #67550, 1927, ex Detroit & Toledo Shore Line #112, bought by S&L 1954.

#87 0-8-0; Baldwin #60833, 1929, ex. Chicago & Illinois Midland #546, ex. Manufacturers Railway of St. Louis #102.

#88 0-8-0: Lima #7713, 1938, ex. Pittsburgh & Lake Erie #8042, ex. New York Central class U-3-K, bought by S&L 1955.

#89 0-8-0; Lima #7702, 1937, ex. Pittsburgh & Lake Erie #8031, ex. New York Central class U-3-k, bought by S&L 1955.

#90 0-8-0; Lima #7682, 1937, ex. Pittsburgh & Lake Erie #8011, ex. New York Central class U-3-k., bought by S&L 1955.

#91 0-8-0; Lima #7700, 1937, ex. Pittsburgh & Lake Erie #8029, ex. New York Central class U-3-k, bought by S&L 1956.

#92 0-8-0: Lima #7711, 1937, ex. Pittsburgh & Lake Erie #8040, ex. New York Central class U-3-k, bought by S&L in 1956.

#93 0-8-0 ALCO (Schenectady) #71894, 1944, ex. Pittsburgh & Lake Erie #8076, ex. New York Central class U-3-L, bought by S&L 1957.

#94 0-8-0; ALCO (Schenectady) #71881, 1944, ex. Pittsburgh & Lake Erie #8061, ex. New York Central class U-3-L, bought by S&L 1957.

#95 0-8-0; ALCO (Schenectady) #71884, 1944, ex. Pittsburgh & Lake Erie #8064, ex. New York Central class U-3-L, bought by S&L 1957.

#100 2-8-2; ALCO (Brooks) #52813, 1918, bought by S&L 1949, scrapped 1958.

#101 2-8-2; ALCO (Brooks) #63571, 1922, ex. Chicago & Eastern Illinois #1943, bought by S&L 1950 and was the most powerful locomotive on the S&L with a tractive effort of 60,000 lb.

#102 2-8-2; ALCO (Schenectady) 59708, 1918, ex. Pere Marquette #1037, ex. New York Central #5113, bought by S&L 1951 and had the largest tender of any locomotive used in Canada.

#103 2-8-2; Baldwin #60336, 1928, ex. Detroit & Toledo Shore Line #26, bought by S&L 1952

#104 2-8-2; Baldwin #60335, 1928, ex. Detroit & Toledo Shore Line #25, bought by S&L 1953.

#105 2-8-2; Lima #7654, 1936, ex. Detroit & Toledo Shore Line #32, bought by S&L, 1954.

#106 2-8-2; ALCO (Brooks) #52547, 1913, ex. Lake Shore & Michigan Southern #4001, ex. New York Central #4001, re. N.Y.C. #7951, re. N.Y.C. #2051, ex. Cumberland Railway & Coal Co. #2051, New York Central #2051 operated on the Canadian Division of the Michigan Central when it was sold to the Cumberland Railway & Coal Co. Its number was not changed. It was exchanged for S&L #43 and numbered S&L #106.

APPENDIX A

S&L Diesels

Road #	Builder	Date	Model	Serial	H.P.	Weight
20	EMC	08/40	40	1134	300	88,000
60	GE	03/49	70-ton	30038	600	137,600
61	Alco-GE	10/40	S 1	69203	660	195,000
200	MLW	/60	RS 23	83289	1000	246,650
201	MLW	/60	RS 23	83290	1000	246,650
202	MLW	/60	RS 23	83291	1000	246,650
203	Alco-GE	09/44	RS 1	71434	1000	242.200
204	Alco-GE	/47	RS 1	75390	1000	240,300
205	Alco-GE	04/45	RS 1	73334	1000	240,300
206	Alco-GE	/44	RS 1	71317	1000	242,200
207	Alco-GE	10/44	RS 1	71436	1000	242,300
208	Alco-GE	08/56	RS 1	75117	1000	242,400
209	Alco-GE	/50	RS 1	77853	1000	243,000
210	Alco-GE	08/50	RS 1	78242	1000	243,000
211	Alco-GE	/51	RS 1	79055	1000	242,000
212	Alco-GE	/51	RS 1	79231	1000	242,000

APPENDIX B

Chronology

Dates and Events of Significance in the History of the S&L Railway

1672 — Nicholas Denys, an early French settler on Cape Breton Island writes of "Mines of coal through the whole extent of my concessions near the seashore". Coal is "mined" by chipping it from cliffs.

1720 — French begin first real coal mines at Cow Bay (Port Morien).

1814 — British engineer, George Stephenson, constructs first practical steam locomotive at Killingworth Colliery, near Newcastle, England.

1818 — In Pictou County, Nova Scotia, two miles of standard gauge train tracks are laid for use with horse-drawn coal cars.

1827 — British firm of Rundell, Bridge and Rundell is granted a monopoly on mining rights in Nova Scotia. They form the General Mining Association [GMA]. Collieries open at Sydney Mines; first train tracks are laid shortly thereafter. Horses provide the motive power.

1839 — Nova Scotia claims the first steam locomotive in use east of Montreal, as the *Samson* takes to the rails on a halfmile track at Pictou.

1851 — A town meeting in Sydney calls on the government to consider Sydney and Louisbourg as termini for the newly proposed "European and North American Railway" across New Brunswick and Nova Scotia.

1854 —The first two locomotives arrive at the GMA's Sydney Mines operations. They are named *Sydney* and *Halifax*.

1858 — The monopoly of the General Mining Association is broken. A flurry of mining activity follows with more than 30 mines opening in the next 36 years, some with their own network of rails connecting them to tidewater.

1864 —A company called the Sydney and Louisbourgh (sic) Railway is incorporated but is not activated. Backers include John Jacob Astor III (1822-90) the great American railroad baron.

1865 —A number of short lines are built from the various collieries to ports in the Glace Bay and Port Caledonia areas. Their exposure to the open ocean makes them difficult and expensive to maintain, as are the loading piers with which they connect.

1870 —The International Coal and Railway Company begins to operate a standard gauge railway from Bridgeport to Sydney. This is the earliest attempt to bring a rail link to Sydney harbour and the international piers.

1871 —The Sydney and Louisburg Coal and Railway Company begins a narrow gauge rail line between the Reserve coal field and Sydney Harbour.

1873 —The Cape Breton Company is formed with the amalgamation of the Glasgow and Cape Breton Coal and Railway Co., the Lorway Coal Co., and the Schooner Pond Coal Co. Frederick Gisborne is one of the driving forces behind the operation. It marks the first attempt to bring a rail terminus to the winter port of Louisburg.

1878 — The Cape Breton Company encounters financial difficulties, becomes bankrupt, and is sold at public auction. The assets are purchased by a group led by Captain David J. Kennelly. The operation is refinanced, re-organized, and renamed the Sydney and Louisburg Coal and Railway Company.

1883 — After only a few years of operation, a forest fire destroys a major section of the S&L line. There had been 32 wooden trestles and 35 large wooden culverts along its 32-mile length.

1884 — The Cape Breton Railway Extension Company is incorporated to build a southern line from the Canso Strait to the port of Louisbourg. By 1903, the line covers the 31-mile distance between Port Hawkesbury and St. Peters. It opens for traffic on September 8, but goes no further.

1885 — Sydney and North Sydney are incorporated.

1886 — Men of the General Mining Association's foundry and shops at Sydney Mines build the locomotive *C.G. Swann*. It is barged across Sydney harbour and serves many years at the Victoria Mines operations.

1888 — A survey reveals that the roadway of the Sydney and Louisburg line has deteriorated to the point where it is unsafe and unusable.

1890 — After a year of political controversy, the trans-island portion of the Intercolonial Railway is completed. The inaugural train arrives in Sydney on October 18. Governor-General Lord Stanley is on board for the ceremony.

1892 — A federal subsidy of $89,000 is offered for the completion of a railway to link the collieries of eastern Cape Breton with the harbours at Sydney and Louisbourg.

1893 — Henry M. Whitney, a Boston-based industrialist, creates the Dominion Coal Company by amalgamating eight of the island's major coal companies. Collectively, their railroad equipment, including 67 miles of roadway, become known as the Dominion Coal Company Railway.

1894 — Government officials and the Dominion Coal Company sign a contract to subsidize the construction of a railway from Sydney to Louisbourg. The cost is $3,200 per mile plus land concessions. Hiram Donkin oversees the construction. Work on the Sydney to Louisbourg line is completed with 39 miles of new tracks. The line links all the major collieries with both seaports. It is the most up-to-date railway in Canada. Its standards of construction are on a par with the newly- completed ICR. A 600-foot coal pier is built at Louisbourg.

1895 — The inaugural run of the S&L takes place on June 17. The date chosen coincides with the 150th anniversary of the 1745 siege of Fortress Louisbourg. The Society of Colonial Wars unveils a monument to honor the soldiers who died at Louisbourg. The two events are combined in a gala celebration. Hundreds ride two special trains to attend the ceremony.

1899 — A new freight pier, later known as the "steel pier" is built at Louisbourg. The Newfoundland ferry *SS Bruce* calls on the winter port with freight and passengers.

1900 — The Dominion Iron and Steel Company steel plant at Sydney begins operations. The S&L gains an important new customer.

1901 — Louisbourg and Glace Bay are incorporated.

1903 — The S&L suffers its two worst disasters in the same year. In the first, a coal train plunges through the open swing bridge at Mira Gut. One man is killed. The second wreck at McAskill's occurs when a work train collides with a coal train. Three men die.

1908 — Special meetings are held in Glace Bay and Sydney with renewed calls for extension of the ICR to Louisbourg, or alternatively for the completion of the southern route from St. Peters to Louisbourg. In May, Cape Breton County Warden H.C.V. LeVatte and Dr. Freeman O'Neil join Cape Breton MPP Dr. Arthur Kendall as delegates to Ottawa in another attempt to get the project completed. It is an election year.

1910 — On September 10, under laws of the Province of Nova Scotia Companies Act, Dominion Coal creates a separate division for its rail operations and incorporates it as a wholly-owned subsidiary to be known as the Sydney and Louisburg Railway Company. It also acquires the Cumberland Coal and Railway Company on mainland Nova Scotia.

1914 — Cape Breton coal and steel production becomes important in the World War I effort. Sydney and Louisbourg play roles as bunkering ports and shippers of war materials.

1927 —The last of the aging wooden hopper cars are weeded out of the S&L system and removed from the line. Those still usable are sold to the Nova Scotia Steel and Coal Company.

1929 — The *North Sydney Herald* reports renewed calls for a completion of the railway from St. Peters to Louisbourg.

1933 — Cape Breton feels the effects of a worldwide depression. Coal production is down and traffic on the S&L Railway is greatly reduced.

1942 —Cape Breton is a major assembly point for ships of the World War II convoys. Availability of coal is a major reason. In a scramble to meet the almost insatiable demand for fuel, coal trains arrive at local shipping piers, sometimes one every 15 minutes. L.H. Cann's Louisbourg Ship Repair Plant employs 150 refitting warships and freighters including those of the Dominion Coal Company fleet. Many mines are at full production.

1949 — The last steam locomotive is built for domestic use in North America.

1951 —100 new hopper cars are delivered to the S&L bringing the total fleet to 1050.

1957 — Hawker Siddley acquires DOSCO.

1959 — The S&L line covers 116.03 miles of tracks; yearly freight totals in the range of 4,000,000 tons; 400 people are employed, and there are 31 locomotives on the roster, one of them built in 1891 is still in service.

1960 — The first four diesel locomotives are brought on line by the S&L. Six more are expected to be in operation by the end of the year. The Mira Station is closed. Stationmaster Alex Ferguson ends a 50-year career with the S&L, 44 of those years as agent at the Mira landmark.

1961 — On September 29, Bill-S19 of the Senate of Canada merges the S&L with the Cumberland Railway Company, another division of the Dominion Steel and Coal Company. Engines No. 88 and 90 are the last steam locomotives on the S&L roster. On November 17 they make their last runs, and are then removed from service.

1962 — Coal shipments at Louisbourg decline to the point where the shipping pier becomes uneconomical to operate. It is dismantled and scrapped. The Dosco coal yard supplying domestic fuel to the town closed a year earlier.

1963 — Passenger service on the S&L is discontinued. The order becomes effective in March.

1967 — The Cumberland Railway makes application to the Board of Transport Commissioners of Canada for abandonment of the railway line from Broughton Junction to Louisbourg. It is a distance of about 12 miles. Hearings are held at Louisbourg. The Cape Breton coal industry is collapsing. The Government of Canada commissions Dr. J.R. Donald to write a report on the "Cape Breton Coal Problem." Hawker Siddley withdraws from the coal fields and announces closure of the Sydney steel plant.

1968 — The Donald Report results in government legislation: Bill C-135 (An Act to Incorporate the Cape Breton Development Corporation). There is no provision for the maintenance of the rail line to Louisbourg. It passes through Parliament, and in March, the Cape Breton Development Corporation (DEVCO) becomes a reality. The S&L is folded into the coal division of DEVCO. It is renamed the Devco Railway. The S&L exists no longer. Within months, the rails to Louisbourg are lifted and sold for their scrap value.

Sources / Bibliography

Almon, Albert, "An Historic Excursion," *Cape Breton Mirror.* (September, 1953).

Belliveau, John Edward, Silver Donald Cameron, and Michael Harrington, *Iceboats to Superferries, An Illustrated History of Marine Atlantic.* St. John's: Breakwater Press, 1992.

Brodie, D.N., "The Old Mira River Steamers," *Cape Breton Mirror*, No. 5, 16-17, 1953.

Bruce, Harry., *Lifeline: The Story of the Atlantic Ferries and Coastal Boats.* Toronto: Macmillian, 1977.

Calder, Fred, "Wreck on the S.&L." and "Before the S.&L." *The Maritime Express*, No. 6, September, 1969.

Calder, J. William, *All Aboard.* Antigonish: Formac Ltd, 1974.

Cameron, Elspeth, *Hugh MacLennan, A Writer's Life*, Toronto: University of Toronto Press, 1981.

Cameron, Gordon. "Notes On Early Coal Mining and Railroading in Cape Breton," unpub. paper, S&L Museum collection.

Cameron, Margaret, *Zion Presbyterian Church, Louisbourg, Nova Scotia.* Louisbourg: Louisbourg Heritage Society, 1991.

Campbell, Anne Marie, "Sydney, Nova Scotia: Shire Town to Steel City," Unpub. paper, Beaton Institute, 1983.

Campbell, Michael R., *The History of Basic Steel Manufacture At Sydney, Nova Scotia.* Sydney: Mining Society of Nova Scotia, 1952.

Centennial Committee, *County of Cape Breton, 1979 Centennial, Sydney: City Printers, 1979.*

Columbus, Sharon, "Mayors of Sydney, 1903-1938," unpub. paper, Beaton Institute, 1983.

Cook, Clayton D., *The End of the Line: the Newfoundland Railway in Pictures,* St. John's: Harry Cuff Publications, 1989.

Cook, Clayton D., *Tales of the Rails: The Newfoundland Railway*, St. John's: Creative Publications, 1991.

Cooley, Thomas M., *The American Railway, Its Construction, Development, Management and Appliances,* Secaucus, N.J.: Castle Book Sales, 1988.

Dobson, George H., *The Transportation Question. Can the St. Lawrence be made a Success by the Utilizing of Sydney and the Nova Scotia Seaboard for Atlantic Transportation?* North Sydney, October 31st, 1876.

Donkin, Hiram, "The Railway System of the Dominion Coal Company Limited," *Canadian Mining Review*, Vol. XIII, No. 8, August, 1894.

Donovan, Kenneth, ed., *Cape Breton at 200, Historical Essays in Honour of the Island's Bicentennial 1785-1985,* Sydney: UCCB Press, 1985.

Donovan, Kenneth, ed., *The Island: New Perspectives on Cape Breton history, 1713-1990.* Fredericton/Sydney: Acadiensis & UCCB Press, 1990.

Doucette, L.J., "55 Years with the Sydney and Louisburg Railway," Leaflet, S&L Railway Historical Society.

Federal Statutes: Railroads. *Chapter 35: An Act to Incorporate the Canso and Louisbourg Railway Company,* July 9, 1892.

Federal Statutes: Railroads. *Chapter 14: An Act to authorize the construction of a railway from the straits of Canso to Louisburg or Sydney as a public work,* June 2, 1886.

Hamilton, William B., *Local History In Atlantic Canada*, Toronto: Macmillian, Toronto, 1974.

Hibbert, Christopher, *The English: A Social History, 1066-1945,* London: Paladin Grafton Books, 1988.

Jackson, Elva E., *North Sydney, Nova Scotia: Windows on the Past*, Belleville: Mika Publishing Company, 1982.

Jefferson, H.B., "100 Percent Steam: 'The Story of the 39-Mile Sydney & Louisburg Railway in Nova Scotia,'" *Railway Magazine,* April, 1960.

Johnson, J.K., The Canadian Directory of Parliament, 1867-1967, Ottawa: Queen's Printer, 1968.

Johnston, A.J.B., "Preserving History: The Commemoration of 18th Century Louisbourg, 1895-1940," *Acadiensis*, Vol. XII, No. 2 (Spring, 1983)

Kennelly, D.J., *The Atlantic Ferry, Louisbourg and Milford Haven*, London: S. Straker and Sons, 1910.

King, J.B., "In the Beginning: The Background of Nova Scotia's Steam Railroads", *The Maritime Express*, No. 11, (December, 1970).

Kyte, Jean, *A History of The First United Church, Louisbourg, Nova Scotia*, Louisbourg: Louisbourg Heritage Society, 1992.

Lockett, E., *Cape Breton Hand-Book and Tourist Guide*, (North Sydney and Sydney, 1890)

Louisbourg Branch of the Women's Institute of Nova Scotia, *History of Modern Louisbourg, 1758-1958*, Reprinted by Louisbourg District Planning Commission, City Printers, Sydney, 1988.

MacBean, Allister W.D., *The Inverness and Richmond Railway*, Halifax: Tennant Publishing House, 1987.

MacDonald, Heather, "The Sydney and Louisbourg Railway, 1895-1968," unpub. paper, Beaton Institute, 1979.

MacGillivray, Don, "Henry Melville Whitney Comes to Cape Breton: The Saga of A Gilded Age Entrepreneur," *Acadiensis,* (Autumn, 1979)

MacKay, Donald, *The People's Railway: A History of Canadian National,* Vancouver/Toronto: Douglas & McIntyre, 1992.

MacNutt, W.S. *The Atlantic Provinces: The Emergence of Colonial Society, 1712-1857,* Toronto: McClelland and Stewart, 1965.

Mellor, John, *The Company Store: James Bryson McLachlan and the Cape Breton Coal Miners, 1900-1925,* New York: Doubleday, 1983.

Mika, Nick and Helma, with Donald M. Wilson, *Illustrated History of Canadian Railways*, Belleville: Mika Publishing, 1986.

Newton, Pamela, *The Cape Breton Book of Days*, Sydney: UCCB Press, 1984.

Noble, Joseph A., *From Cab To Caboose: Fifty Years of Railroading*, Norman, Oklahoma: University of Oklahoma Press, 1964.

O'Shea, William, with Helen A. O'Shea & Jean Kyte, *Louisbourg Streets*, Louisbourg: Louisbourg Heritage Society, 1990.

O'Shea, William, *The Louisbourg Brass Bands*, Louisbourg: Louisbourg Heritage Society, 1991.

O'Shea, William & Helen, *Stella Maris Roman Catholic Church, Louisbourg, Nova Scotia,* Louisbourg: Louisbourg Heritage *Society, 1993.*

Parker, John P., *Cape Breton Ships And Men*, Aylesbury, England: Hazell Watson & Viney Ltd., 1967.

Pole, Gordon, "Gisborne: A Pioneer of the Telegraphic Link," in "Dreamers & Doers," *Atlantic Intercommunications*, Volume 2, No. 2, June 1991.

"The Prosperity of Cape Breton," *Canadian Mining Review*, Vol. XIX, No. 9, September, 1900.

Ripley, Ralph Wayne, "Social and Cultural Implications of Industrialization and Urbanization in Cape Breton County, 1893-1914, (B.A. Thesis, St. Francis Xavier University, 1979).

Snow, Charles L., *Petition and Letter of the Great American & European Short Line Railway In Regard To The Completion of its Air Line from Montreal to Louisbourg*, Ottawa, April 18, 1883.

Stevens, G.R. *Canadian National Railways, Volume 2, Towards the Inevitable, 1896-1922,* Toronto: Clarke, Irwin, 1962.

Tennyson, Brian, and Don Macgillivray, eds., *Cape Breton Historical Essays*, Sydney: College of Cape Breton Press, 1981.

Tennyson, Brian E., ed., *Impressions of Cape Breton*, Sydney: UCCB Press, 1986.

Vernon, C.W., *Cape Breton Canada*, Toronto: Nation Publishing, 1903.

Willmot, Elizabeth A., *Meet Me at the Station*, Toronto: Gage Publishing, 1976.

Woods, Shirley E., *Cinders & Saltwater: The Story of Atlantic Canada's Railways, Halifax: Nimbus Publishing, 1992.*

"Working on the S&L Railroad," Parts One and Two, *Cape Breton's Magazine*, Cape Breton Magazine, Issues No. 28 and 29.